D1453657

The Simple *Guide to* College Admission & Financial Aid™

How to Select the Right College

Applying for College Admission

Writing the College Essay

The Financial Aid Process Made Easy

VERNON COLLEGE LIBRARY

Anne M. St. Pierre & Danielle M. Printz

Address questions and comments to *The Simple Guide to College Admission & Financial Aid*, c/o The Simple Guide Company, Inc., P.O. Box 8474, Portland, Maine 04104. Submit your comments or questions via email to: <info@simpleguidetocollege.com>.

Visit *The Simple Guide to College Admission and Financial Aid* on the web at <www.simpleguidetocollege.com>.

The authors have sought to ensure that the information contained in this book is accurate as of the time of publication. Because policies, Federal Student Financial Aid, costs and statistics may change from time to time, readers should verify important information with the colleges or universities of interest or the Federal Student Aid Center.

The Simple Guide to College Admission and Financial Aid

Copyright © 2006 by The Simple Guide Company, Inc.
All rights reserved. Printed in the United States of America. No part of this book may be used or reproduced in any manner whatsoever without written permission.

ISBN 0-9772143-1-1

The SAT® and CSS Financial Aid PROFILE® are registered trademarks of the College Board.
The ACTAssessment® is a registered trademark of ACT Inc.

Introduction

Thinking about going to college? **_The Simple Guide to College Admission & Financial Aid_** can help you get there.

Over the past few years, your experiences in school, your job and community have provided you with many opportunities to learn more about your career interests and colleges you might want to attend. Now, throughout the college application and financial aid processes, you have a comprehensive resource - **_The Simple Guide to College Admission & Financial Aid_** - to help you through the necessary steps along the way.

Getting an early start on the college process is a great advantage for you. The "Guide" can help you choose the right school, as well as provide important information on applying for admission and financial aid - everything you need to make the college and financial aid processes easier, successful and less stressful.

So, what are you waiting for - read on!

Contents

Senior Calendar

September

❑ Narrow your list of college choices to about 3 – 9 schools. Use the *College Information Worksheets* beginning on p. 24 to help you.

❑ Contact colleges or visit websites. Make a note of application deadlines on the *College Information Worksheets*.

❑ Save time and complete the Common Application at <**www.commonapp.org**>. You may be able to complete one application and send it to several colleges.

❑ Register for the SAT Reasoning Test® and/or SAT Subject Tests® or the ACT®. You may qualify for a fee waiver – this means you may not have to pay the test fee(s). Check with your school counselor.

❑ Does the school to which you are applying require that you take the SAT Subject Tests®? If so, which subject tests are required? Be sure you check admission requirements.

❑ Plan on participating in college athletics? Contact college coaches. Register for NCAA Clearinghouse at <**www.ncaaclearinghouse.net**>.

❑ Schedule college visits and interviews. Call soon for an appointment.

❑ If you are completing applications for Early Decision or Early Action, know your deadlines and meet with your school counselor early.

October

❑ Check with each college to which you are applying to determine if the CSS/Financial Aid PROFILE® is required. The PROFILE is not a free form, but you may qualify for a fee waiver. You can complete the PROFILE online at <**www.collegeboard.com**>.

❑ Ask 1-3 teachers to write you a letter of recommendation. Be sure to give them *at least* 2 weeks advanced notice.

❑ If you are submitting the Common Application to schools, be sure to download the School Report and Midyear forms from <**www.commonapp.org**>. Give the forms to your school counselor to complete.

❑ Write your college essay. Ask your English teacher to proofread it for you.

❑ Prepare for the SAT or ACT.

❑ Check in with your parents and your school counselor and inform them of the schools to which you are applying.

❑ Take the SAT Reasoning Test and/or SAT Subject Tests (if necessary) or the ACT.

❑ If you have not already done so, call to schedule college visits and interviews.

November

- ❑ Review and revise your college essay(s). Ask your English teacher to read your essay.
- ❑ Complete your college applications. Make copies of your work.
- ❑ If you are submitting the Common Application to schools, be sure to download any supplements required by specific schools. You can find out which schools require supplements at <**www.commonapp.org**>.
- ❑ Perform a scholarship search – start in your guidance office for local and state scholarship information. (Note: Scholarship applications do not cost money. NEVER pay to apply for any scholarship). Use the *Keeping Track of Your Scholarships* worksheet on p. 62 to keep you on course.
- ❑ Many deadlines for Early Action/Decision are in November and December. Play it safe. Be sure admission applications, test scores, academic records, recommendations and other requirements are received by colleges prior to deadlines.
- ❑ If you are planning to play a sport in college, have you registered with the NCAA Clearinghouse yet? Pick up the paper form at your athletic director's office or your guidance office. You can apply online at <**www.ncaaclearinghhouse.net**>. There is a fee to apply. Ask your athletic director if you qualify for a fee waiver.

December

- ❑ Finish your applications. *Be sure to proofread and proofread again*. Make copies of your applications. Mail applications, supporting materials along with the application fee or fee waiver. Contact your school counselor to find out if you are eligible for a fee waiver.
- ❑ Be sure your school counselor knows where to send your transcripts. If you are submitting the Common Application to schools, remember to download the School Report and Mid-Year Report forms for your counselor to complete.
- ❑ Research national, state and local scholarships. Update your *Keeping Track of Your Scholarships* worksheet to keep you on course.
- ❑ Check with the guidance office for local scholarships. Search for more scholarships at <**www.fastweb.com**> or <**www.theoldschool.org**>.
- ❑ Reminder: Have you visited those schools yet?
- ❑ Financial Aid: Register for your FAFSA PIN at <**www.pin.ed.gov**>.
- ❑ Financial Aid Workshop: Plan to attend your state's **College Goal Sunday** event. This is a free workshop organized by the National Association of Student Financial Aid Administrators. This workshop will help you complete your FAFSA. To find out if College Goal Sunday is offered in your state, visit <**www.nasfaa.org**> click on College Goal Sunday and then click on your state.
- ❑ Highly selective institutions usually have earlier application deadlines. Be sure you meet deadlines. Missed deadlines are missed opportunities to be considered for admission.
- ❑ Check with your high school to find out when Financial Aid Night is; plan to attend this important event with your parents.

January

☐ Attend your high school's Financial Aid Night.

☐ Complete the FAFSA as soon as possible after January 1st. You can complete the FAFSA paper form or apply online at <**www.fafsa.ed.gov**>. Applying online is easier and will save four weeks of processing time.

☐ Check with each school's Financial Aid Office to determine whether you must complete additional financial aid forms.

☐ Continue your research of scholarships.

☐ Still hanging onto college applications? Mail them!

☐ If you or your parents are usually late-tax-filers - not this year! You and your parents should file as soon as possible. A school may need a copy of your income tax documents prior to making a financial aid award to you. Filing your taxes late delays the entire financial aid process.

February

☐ If you still have not completed your FAFSA, complete it now!

☐ Scholarship application deadlines are approaching – do not miss them!

☐ Deadlines, deadlines! Have you mailed your college applications on time?

☐ Your completed FAFSA will generate a Student Aid Report (SAR). Review your SAR for accuracy and for verification. If your SAR has been selected for verification, send income tax documents to the school as soon as possible.

March

☐ Complete the remainder of your local, state, regional and national level scholarship applications. Note deadlines!

☐ Many schools send financial aid award letters at this time. Use these letters to complete the *College Cost Comparison* worksheets on pp. 94 & 95. This may assist you in determining the best financial aid award for you. Be sure to review the award letters carefully. You have to respond to financial aid award letters by a deadline, so do not delay or your offer of aid could be lost.

☐ Have not heard from those highly selective colleges regarding admission? Do not worry just yet. Usually these schools send acceptance letters at the end of this month or beginning of April.

April

❑ Review your financial aid packages and compare with the college's Cost of Attendance. Call the colleges' Financial Aid Office if you have questions.

❑ Determine which college you plan to attend and send in your deposit. Selecting a college is an important and sometimes difficult decision! Discuss this decision with your parents and school counselor.

May

❑ Complete housing forms sent to you by the colleges. Some schools have limited residence hall space, which is usually first-come first-served.

❑ Inform your guidance office of your college decision.

❑ Complete and submit your Federal Stafford Loan and/or Perkins Loan applications if necessary, and complete the Entrance Counseling requirement.

❑ Find a summer job and save money for college.

❑ Be sure to sign-up for your college's new student orientation. New student orientation events usually take place during the summer or immediately prior to the start of classes. It is important to attend because you will select and register for your college classes during the event.

June

❑ Use the summer to purchase items you will need for your new life at college! Review *What to Bring to College* on p. 100.

❑ Continue to save money for college.

❑ Enjoy your summer!

College Selection

Choosing the Right College

You probably already know there are many reasons why it is important to continue your education. No matter what your career goals are, a college education can help you reach them. A college education can also give you more career options, personal satisfaction, higher income, knowledge, experiences and opportunities that will enrich your life and help you achieve your dreams. Whether you plan to attend a four-year college or university, community college, or technical school, or are unsure at this point, this section will give you the guidelines for selecting colleges, as well as the necessary information you will need to apply for admission.

If you have not explored many colleges by now, you will learn that there are many options when it comes to choosing colleges – like community and technical colleges, small private colleges and large state universities. Each type of college has advantages and benefits, and there are many resources that can help you choose the school that is right for you.

An excellent (and free) resource for your initial college search is the U.S. Department of Education's website Student Aid on the Web at **<www.studentaid.ed.gov>**. This non-profit site also has a great deal of career, college and financial aid information. In fact, when you log in and input your student information, when you are ready to file your Free Application for Federal Student Aid (FAFSA) you can do so from this site without the need for typing your information again. You can also complete a college search by visiting the College Board's website at **<www.collegeboard.com>**, and check out college rankings at the Princeton Review's website **<www.princetonreview.com>**. Before you begin your online search, you might want to develop a list of your priorities and identify characteristics of a college that appeal to you. For example, some students may want to attend a small school, or search for schools with a specific sport, program/major, admissions criteria and reputation, etc. Review information about each school so that you can make an informed decision.

For more information about colleges, check with your high school – they may have career and college information computer programs to which you will have access. Consult with teachers, friends or professionals who may have attended a college you are considering. When researching colleges, you can search schools by state, majors and programs, campus size and athletics, just to mention a few.

So, where do you start? Begin by making a list of your colleges from your search that matches your criteria. The following considerations may help you to decide what type of school is best for you and then begin your college search.

Types of Schools

Researching school types will help you narrow your potential list of institutions and programs to which to apply. Spend some time thinking about what college or university may be a good fit for you. Below are descriptions of types of schools:

College - an institution that offers students a curriculum resulting in a four-year bachelor degree in a specific program.

University - an institution that may be similar to a college, usually compromised of several colleges (such as college of engineering, etc.) and in addition, may offer a graduate degree beyond a bachelor degree.

Community College - an institution that provides two-year programs of study towards a certificate or an associate degree. A community college can be for the student who transfers to a four-year college or university, or for the student who wants a specialized training program for a specific occupation.

Vocational or Technical School - an institution that offers career-oriented programs in certain specialized occupations. These schools offer intensive courses of study that may take weeks, months or several years to complete, depending on the academic program.

United States Military Academies - are four-year institutions that are part of the military services. Like other colleges and universities, the academies consider your application materials carefully. Admission to all of the United States Military Academies is highly selective. Check the websites for current eligibility criteria, admissions requirements and information. All, except the United States Coast Guard Academy, require applicants to obtain congressional nominations for admission. Instructions and sources for congressional nominations are outlined at each website.

United States Air Force Academy - <*www.usafa.edu*>
United States Coast Guard Academy - <*www.cga.edu*>
United States Merchant Marine Academy - <*usmma.edu*>
United States Military Academy at West Point - <*www.usma.edu*>
United States Naval Academy - <*www.usna.edu*>

Characteristics of Schools

Prior to starting your online search, you may wish to identify characteristics of a college that appeal to you. For example, you may wish to search for small schools, colleges with a specific sport or program/major, admission criteria, reputation, etc. Research each school so you can decide if you wish to apply.

Academic Programs & Majors

You may already have a career goal in mind; if so, be sure to research schools that offer that program or major. No major? No problem. If you are undecided at the moment, do not worry. While at college, you will have many opportunities to explore careers and majors before choosing one.

Admissions Difficulty Level

Searching by admissions entrance difficulty level may be important to you. Match your academic experience, grade point average, etc. with a school's admissions criteria. For example, if you wish to attend a highly selective school, make sure you have the grades, required coursework, test scores, and other requirements to be a competitive applicant.

Location

City life? Country charm? College campuses can range from several city blocks to a few acres in the country, to everything in between. Are you planning to visit home often? Do you prefer rolling hills, mountains, skyscrapers, warm or cold weather? If location matters to you, then be sure to research colleges that will provide you with the environment that suits you.

Does Size Matter?

College campuses can range from a few hundred students to thousands. You may know everyone on-campus or see a new face every day. The number of students at a college can sometimes affect your experiences on a campus or in the classroom. For example, at a large school, you may find yourself in a class with 100+ students. At a smaller school, you may attend class with just a handful of classmates. Which environment appeals more to you?

Financial Aid

Most students require some sort of financial aid to attend college. Research your schools carefully and determine the total cost of attending the school (tuition, room and board, fees, books) but *do not let the price tag scare you*. Financial aid is designed to assist students throughout college. A couple of tips: 1) Public schools are usually less expensive than private schools and 2) state public schools are usually less expensive for residents than out-of-state students and 3) some highly selective private schools have larger amounts of money to help pay for the cost of school. When researching financial aid, find out what the college's "median" financial aid award is for incoming freshman. If you need financial aid to attend college, this will give you an idea of affordability.

Campus Life

Do you want to be part of a fraternity or sorority? How about the school newspaper, basketball team, marching band or chess club? What is the campus social life like? Your college search should consider campus life, activities and opportunities in which you might like to participate.

Still Not Sure?

Keep in mind that choosing a college is not just about choosing where you are going to spend the next two to four years of your life. It is about setting life and career goals and figuring out what college or program can best help you reach those goals. And remember, you do not have to know exactly what career you want at the moment. Many high school seniors are unsure about their career path when they enter college; also, they might change their minds while in college. So if you have not figured it all out yet, it is ok; there is plenty of time.

FREE RESOURCES FOR YOUR COLLEGE SEARCH

There are many FREE resources that can help you choose the school that is right for you. Figure out what traits are important to you and what the general requirements for admission to college are, such as academic major or program, location, size, financial aid, campus life, type of school, etc. Check out the following websites for college searches. College searches should always be FREE.

<www.studentaid.ed.gov>
<www.petersons.com>
<www.collegeboard.com>
<www.princetonreview.com>

Sample Letter to Request Information from a College

Your Name
Your Address
City, State Zip Code

Date

Dear Admissions Officer,

*I am a high school senior at **[Your High School]** and will be enrolling in college next year. I am interested in attending your school and would like to receive information about admissions requirements, application deadlines and financial aid.*

***[I am planning to major in_____] [I am currently undecided about a major]** and would appreciate any information you could send about requirements, programs, and possible scholarships.*

Please send the information to the address above. Your time and consideration are greatly appreciated.

Sincerely,

Sign Your Letter

Your Name
Your Email Address

Summary

- A college education will give you more options, personal satisfaction, a higher income, knowledge, experiences and opportunities.

- Each type of college has advantages and benefits. There many resources that can assist you with your college search. An excellent (and free) resource for your initial college search is the U.S. Department of Education's website Student Aid on the Web at <www.studentaid.ed.gov>.

- Develop a list of your priorities and identify characteristics of a college that appeal to you based on the type of school, as well as academic program or major, admissions difficulty, location, campus size and campus life.

"To Do" List

- ❏ Write a list of priorities and college characteristics that appeal to you. Use the Notes section in the back of the book.

- ❏ Check out college search resources at your high school, such as computer programs or college handbooks.

- ❏ Do your online college search at any of the following sites:

    <www.studentaid.ed.gov>
    <www.petersons.com>
    <www.collegeboard.com>
    <www.princetonreview.com>

The Application Process

Getting Ready To Apply

Once you have developed a list of colleges that match your preferences, the next step is to refine your list to be sure you have more than a few appropriate options. For example, apply to at least two colleges where you *know* you will be accepted and will receive adequate financial aid. After all, the goal is to go to college, right? If you have researched and planned well, you will have plenty of options when the time comes to make your college decision. If not, you may have limited your options. By applying to only one or two schools that were unrealistic (i.e. long shots for acceptance or good financial aid awards), you may find that you were not accepted or cannot afford to go. That is why applying to appropriate schools is important to your future. There is no substitute for good planning based on realistic expectations and a sound strategy.

One way to make sure you have allowed yourself as many options as possible is to carefully consider where you will apply. You can do this by researching your schools' admissions criteria and financial aid programs. Many answers to your questions will be on the college's website or literature, but call the college if you have questions that are not answered at the site or in the literature you receive. The following guidelines will help you create plenty of possibilities for a successful college admission.

Apply to 3 to 9 schools

It is as easy as 1-2-3. Use the ***College Information Worksheets*** on pp. 24-26 to help you research your schools.

1. **Apply to 1-2 "REACH" schools**
   (where you may have a 50/50 chance of acceptance)

2. **Apply to 2 - 4 "MID-RANGE" schools**
   (where you will likely be accepted)

3. **Apply to 2 - 3 "SAFETY" schools**
   (where you know for sure that you will be accepted
   and can afford to go)

How do you know what is a reach school and a safety school? Be realistic and honest with yourself – be sure to check the admissions requirements at each school you are applying to and make certain you have met all the admissions criteria/requirements. Weigh all the information you have received to make your decision whether or not to apply to a college. Remember, choosing a college can be one of the most important and difficult decisions you will make.

Schools You Are Thinking About   *(circle one)*

1. _____   Reach   Mid-Range   Safety

2. _____   Reach   Mid-Range   Safety

3. _____   Reach   Mid-Range   Safety

4. _____   Reach   Mid-Range   Safety

5. _____   Reach   Mid-Range   Safety

6. _____   Reach   Mid-Range   Safety

7. _____   Reach   Mid-Range   Safety

8. _____   Reach   Mid-Range   Safety

9. _____   Reach   Mid-Range   Safety

Is Your List Too Long? Not Long Enough?

If you are still struggling with your list of schools, you might consider visiting the colleges. This is a great way to find out if you and the school are a good match. Besides, visiting a campus gives you a "feel" for the environment. It gives you the opportunity to view the community, campus environment and facilities, and talk with students and faculty. A visit gives you the chance to ask questions about admissions, financial aid, and student life on campus.

While you are visiting a school, you will want to experience as much of the college as possible during your visit. So, when you get to campus, here are some suggestions for your visit:

1. **Tour the campus.** Even if you visited the college before, you may have a different experience this time; there may also have been many changes to the campus since your last visit. For example, perhaps there are new programs, classrooms or a field house, etc.

2. **Admissions interview.** Even if a school does not require an interview, requesting one will show the admissions reps that you are interested in the school. Aside from your college essay, your interview

gives you the best opportunity to make a good impression. Call the college to schedule an interview prior to your visit. Be prepared to answer many questions as well as ask some of your own (*see **Questions To Ask a College Admissions Counselor** on p. 40*).

3. **Meet with the Financial Aid Office.** It is very important to connect with the Financial Aid Office at the school. You will have the opportunity to ask important questions, such as "What is the average financial aid package for a freshman?" (*see **Questions To Ask Financial Aid Officers** on p. 67*).

4. **Have Lunch on Campus.** You may be living on a campus for two to four years and eating is an essential part of college life. Some colleges will even pay for your meal during your visit.

5. **Meet with a coach.** If you are interested in a certain sport or activity, talking with a coach or athletic department representative can be helpful. Besides being a student who will succeed academically, colleges want students who will be involved in campus activities. Be sure to set up these appointments in advance of your visit.

6. **Check out the dorms.** Is it loud or quiet, dirty or clean? Does it smell like dirty socks or as fresh as a spring rain? This is the best way to see for yourself if it is a place you can live for the next few years. Additionally, check out the variety of housing options available to you at the school. Is there off-campus housing, are dorms co-ed, are there dorms for specific majors, apartments or suites?

Having a clear picture of what a college is all about will help you make your decision. In fact, your campus visit might be just the start of great experiences yet to come! Contact the college's admissions office to help you schedule your college visit.

Each college has their own admission process

As far as the admissions process is concerned, you will need to know the following about your schools.

Is the school considered Highly Selective? Schools that are highly selective sometimes have application deadlines as early as December 1st. To be considered by regular admissions standards, be sure to file your application during the fall of your senior year. Decisions are mailed to applicants from March to mid-April.

Does the school have Rolling Admission? Rolling admission can benefit some students (like those who procrastinate). At schools with rolling admissions, applications are reviewed as the admission file for each student is completed – until all slots for enrollment are full. Decisions regarding admissions are made on an ongoing basis.

Will you apply for Early Admission? Some schools have both early and regular admission deadlines. For early admission consideration, students sometimes apply as early as their junior year of high school or early in the early fall of their senior year. Usually, this is an option for honor or advanced placement level students.

Thinking about Early Decision? This is another option for some students. To be considered for early decision, students apply to their first choice of a college early in the fall (usually by November 1st) of their senior year and agree by contract to enter that college if offered admission. Beware, some schools will not commit to financial aid packages this early in the year . . . and if you need aid to go to college, this might not be the option for you.

Are you interested in a January Admission? Some schools have an option where students are admitted as freshmen and begin study in the middle of the academic year (instead of the fall). Often, this is a way for students who have been "wait listed," which means the student was not accepted for the fall semester, but put on a waiting list to gain admission. If you are wait listed, the college may offer you admission for the second semester (January).

What is Deferred Admission? If you applied and were accepted to a school, but cannot attend as planned, you might be given the opportunity to delay or defer your enrollment for a semester or sometimes up to a year. Check with your school to find out if they offer deferred admission. A deposit is often required by the college to reserve your place.

What about Open Admission? Schools with open admission options offer acceptance to all qualified applicants until the maximum enrollment number is reached. Because there may be a finite amount of admissions openings available for incoming freshmen, submitting your application materials early will help the possibility of your acceptance.

Your College Application File

In addition to the school's own application form, many of your schools will likely require additional information to complete your application file. Your application file might include any of the following items:

1) Admission application
2) Application fee *
3) Transcripts
4) Essay
5) Letters of recommendation
6) Test scores
7) Supplemental information (i.e. portfolio, etc.)
8) Admissions interview
9) Financial aid application

Hint

Save $$
Ask your colleges and school counselor about college application fee waivers!

Remember to keep copies of all information you submit.

* A Note about College Application Fees: Eligible students can receive *college application fee waivers* for participating colleges. These waivers eliminate or reduce the cost of your college applications. So, ask your school counselor or guidance office if you are eligible. Call your colleges for more information on fee waivers. You could save hundreds of dollars!

Know the application fee, deadlines and admissions criteria for each of the schools on your list so that you can be sure you have met all application requirements of the school. Colleges will not process your information until your application file is complete.

Asking for Recommendations

Most colleges and universities require one to three recommendations from each applicant. Your recommendations give schools more information about you that is not reflected in your transcript, grade point average or application. So, consider carefully whom you will ask to write your recommendations. How do you go about getting recommendations?

1) **Ask Your Teachers**. Find a teacher who knows you well. A teacher who knows your performance as a student and who can write an honest recommendation about your character and ability is a good person to ask. It could be a teacher you had your junior or senior year. If you are thinking about a specific field of study, it makes good sense to ask a teacher from that department. Choose someone you feel confident will give you a good recommendation. Be realistic. Do

not expect a teacher to write wonderful things about your performance if you received a D in class!

2) **Timing is Everything.** Ask teachers early enough in the year (September) to give them plenty of time to write your recommendation and give you time to meet application deadlines.

3) **After a Teacher Agrees to Write Your Recommendation.** If a teacher agrees to write your recommendation, be sure to give them the necessary materials to complete the process, such as the recommendation form and an addressed stamped envelope for each school. Some schools have their own recommendation forms. The Common Application has a Teacher Evaluation form that you can download from <**www.commonapp.org**>.

4) **Thank You.** Be sure to send a thank you note to every teacher that writes a recommendation for you. Remember, they are doing you a favor by writing your recommendation. A thank you note is both appropriate and necessary. Additionally, writing a thank you note continues a positive impression of the student.

How Colleges Make Their Decisions

Colleges will carefully review your application and supporting materials (essay, recommendations, etc.). Your application is an opportunity for admissions representatives to learn more about your strengths, aspirations, priorities, values and skills. It is important that you give as much information about yourself as you can on your application. This will help admissions distinguish you from another applicant, especially if the applicant pool is competitive.

The way that your application is evaluated varies from school-to-school, but in general, most schools evaluate your application by reviewing academic history (grades, classes, rank), test scores, letters of recommendation, and your essay. As you know, some schools are more selective than others. How do you know the selectivity level of a school? Ask the admissions office about their acceptance rate. Schools that have a selectivity rate below 30% are considered selective. This means that only about 30% of applicants are accepted for admission (Harvard University's admission rate is only about 10-12%). Selectivity levels range from those that accept all qualified applicants to the most selective schools, like Harvard, that accept only 10-12% of applicants. Selective or not, the most important piece of your application is your academic record of the classes you have taken in high school and the grades you

> **Hint**
>
> **What About Grades?**
>
> Sometimes a student's transcript shows a dramatic decline in grades for a term or even a year. If there is a special circumstance that may have contributed to low grades for a term/year (i.e. medical, move, divorce, etc.) the student should write a letter or request an interview with an admission rep to explain.

received. However, earning a 4.0 grade point average in basic or general level high school classes is not going to meet the admission criteria at selective schools. Your application for admission will likely be denied. Selective schools look for students who have taken challenging classes for four years of high school such as college preparatory, honors and advanced placement classes. Additionally, these selective schools review your supporting material much more closely. Most schools will look at the following when reviewing your application file:

- Grades
- Class Rank
- Interview
- Courses Taken
- SAT/ACT Test Scores
- Major to which you applied
- Recommendation Letters

- Special Talents and Skills
- Community Service
- Extracurricular Activities
- Ethnicity
- Geographic Location
- Alumni Relationships

Selective schools are looking for students who will make positive contributions to classes, the college and the campus environment. Again, if you are applying to selective schools, it is important that you give as much information about yourself as you can. These schools are looking for something unique and rare about your application – something that sets you apart from other applicants. For example, including on your application information about your interests, ways that you have participated in your community or overcome a specific barrier to achieve a goal are good ways to tell the admissions office more about you.

PERSONAL INFORMATION

Most college applications will ask you for personal information. Use the next two worksheets to record your data. When you are ready to apply, all of the information will be at your fingertips!

Standardized Test Information

Test date of:

SAT Reasoning Test	_____ month _____ year	Total Score:_____
SAT Subject Test(s)	_____ month _____ year	Total Score:_____
ACT	_____ month _____ year	Total Score:_____
TOEFL	_____ month _____ year	Total Score:_____

Are you a TRiO or GEAR UP Student? Check your program below:

_____ Educational Talent Search
_____ Upward Bound
_____ Educational Opportunity Center
_____ GEAR UP

Additional Information on your College Application

Is there any additional information about you or your family that may be helpful as the school evaluates your application?

1. If you are the first in your family to attend college, this is important information for your schools to know.
2. If you are a TRiO or GEAR UP student, write about your participation in the program.
3. Did your grades change dramatically for a term or year? Explain why.

_____
_____
_____
_____
_____
_____
_____
_____
_____
_____
_____
_____

Hobbies and/or Special Interests

_____
_____
_____

VC LIBRARY

Employment Experience
(indicate number of hours per week, include summer work)

Grades participated
9   10 11 12

❏ ❏ ❏ ❏

❏ ❏ ❏ ❏

❏ ❏ ❏ ❏

❏ ❏ ❏ ❏

Community & Volunteer Work Activities
(indicate number of hours per week)

Grades participated
9   10 11 12

❏ ❏ ❏ ❏

❏ ❏ ❏ ❏

❏ ❏ ❏ ❏

❏ ❏ ❏ ❏

School Clubs & Activities
Offices held

Grades participated
9   10 11 12

❏ ❏ ❏ ❏

❏ ❏ ❏ ❏

❏ ❏ ❏ ❏

❏ ❏ ❏ ❏

Honors & Awards
Offices held

Grades participated
9   10 11 12

❏ ❏ ❏ ❏

❏ ❏ ❏ ❏

❏ ❏ ❏ ❏

Music/Theatre/Visual Arts
(indicate productions, instrument played)
Offices held

Grades participated
9   10 11 12

❏ ❏ ❏ ❏

❏ ❏ ❏ ❏

❏ ❏ ❏ ❏

Athletics
Position, Varsity Letter

Grades Participated
9   10 11 12

❏ ❏ ❏ ❏

❏ ❏ ❏ ❏

❏ ❏ ❏ ❏

Completing Your College Applications

You are ready to apply to college! Let's get started.

It is important that you have selected the right schools to which to apply. If you have not chosen your schools yet, please complete the first section of this guide – *College Selection*.

Hint

Admission applications for first year students can be found on a college's website usually under the Undergraduate Admission or Prospective Student sections.

Where do you get college applications? Most college websites have applications you can download, or you can get them at college fairs, during college visits, or even through your high school guidance office. There are many college search sites such as <**www.studentaid.ed.gov**> and <**www.petersons.com**> that can help you find specific college websites where you can download applications for admissions.

The Common Application - Several Colleges, One Application

Many private colleges and public universities accept what is called the Common Application <**www.commonapp.org**>. The Common Application allows you to submit the same application to different schools – you only have to complete the application once! So, if some of your schools accept the Common Application, your life just got a little easier. As a matter of fact, there are some institutions that accept *only* the Common Application. You can find out which schools accept the Common Application by reviewing the list of schools on the Common Application website.

Do not make the mistake of completing only the application portion of the Common Application. There are many other pieces to it, including Teacher Evaluations, a School Report, and a Midyear Report. Additionally, there may be supplemental forms required for some of your schools. Follow the instructions on the Common Application website to make certain you did not overlook these additional forms or supplements.

College application fee waivers

Remember, eligible students can receive college application fee waivers for participating colleges. These waivers eliminate (or reduce) the cost of submitting your college applications. Get the details from your school counselor today. You could save hundreds of dollars!

Summary

- Do your homework about the colleges that may interest you. After all, the goal is to go to college, right? Check the admission criteria at each school to which you are applying and make certain you meet all admissions requirements.

- Develop a list of colleges that match your preferences and refine your list to be sure you have more than a few options of appropriate schools.

- Apply to 3 to 9 schools: 1 to 2 Reach Schools
      2 to 4 Mid-Range Schools
      2 to 3 Safety Schools

"To Do" List

- ❏ Refine your list of schools to include reach, mid-range **and** safety schools.

- ❏ Complete the **Personal Information** worksheets. This will help you when you are ready to complete your college applications.

- ❏ Visit the colleges that interest you.

- ❏ Ask your teachers for recommendations.

- ❏ Know all admissions application policies and **deadlines**. Your college admission application file may not be considered complete without all of the following possible requirements:

  - Admission application
  - Application fee
  - Transcripts
  - Essay
  - Letters of recommendation
  - Test scores
  - Supplemental information (i.e. portfolio, etc.)
  - Admissions interview
  - Financial aid application

College Information Worksheet - REACH SCHOOLS

Details & Admission:	Reach 1	Reach 2	Reach 3
Number of Students			
Location			
Campus setting (rural, urban)			
Acceptance rate			
Grade Point Average			
SAT or ACT minimum			
SAT Subject Tests required			
Placement Test required			
Cost of Attendance			

Your evaluation:			
Meet admission requirements			
Order of preference			

Application Checklist:			
Application deadline			
Application fee			
Application fee waiver			
Recommendations			
Essay			
Interview/Visit			

Other:			

Reach: Student is uncertain of acceptance & adequate financial aid.

Mid-range: Student is partially certain of acceptance & adequate financial aid.

Safety: Student is certain of acceptance & adequate financial aid.

College Information Worksheet - MID-RANGE SCHOOLS

Details & Admission:	Mid-Range 1	Mid-Range 2	Mid-Range 3
Number of Students			
Location			
Campus setting (rural, urban)			
Acceptance rate			
Grade Point Average			
SAT or ACT minimum			
SAT Subject Tests required			
Placement Test required			
Cost of Attendance			

Your evaluation:			
Meet admission requirements			
Order of preference			

Application Checklist:			
Application deadline			
Application fee			
Application fee waiver			
Recommendations			
Essay			
Interview/Visit			

Other:			

Reach: Student is uncertain of acceptance & adequate financial aid.

Mid-range: Student is partially certain of acceptance & adequate financial aid.

Safety: Student is certain of acceptance & adequate financial aid.

College Information Worksheet - SAFETY SCHOOLS

	Safety 1	Safety 2	Safety 3
Details & Admission:			
Number of Students			
Location			
Campus setting (rural, urban)			
Acceptance rate			
Grade Point Average			
SAT or ACT minimum			
SAT Subject Tests required			
Placement Test required			
Cost of Attendance			
Your evaluation:			
Meet admission requirements			
Order of preference			
Application Checklist:			
Application deadline			
Application fee			
Application fee waiver			
Recommendations			
Essay			
Interview/Visit			
Other:			

Reach: Student is uncertain of acceptance & adequate financial aid.

Mid-range: Student is partially certain of acceptance & adequate financial aid.

Safety: Student is certain of acceptance & adequate financial aid.

Keeping Track of Your College Applications

So far, you have (1) selected the schools to which you want to apply, (2) completed the *College Information Worksheets* to select your schools, and (3) requested each school's application information. Now, use the worksheets on the following pages to sort and keep track of your applications and materials needed to complete your application file at all of your schools.

School   ❏ Reach   ❏ Mid-Range   ❏ Safety

School Name: _____

Contact: _____ **Telephone:** _____

Application Deadline: _____

Admission Interview?   Yes   No   **Date scheduled:** _____

Portfolio required?   Yes   No   **Requirements:** _____

Open House or College Tour/Visit Date: _____

Application type (check one)	Date sent	Method
❏ School Specific Application Form:	_____	Hard copy mailed
	_____	Online submission
❏ Common Application:	_____	Hard copy mailed
	_____	Online submission
❏ Common Application Supplement:	_____	

Standardized Test Scores	Required		Date Taken
❏ SAT Reasoning Test	Yes	No	_____
❏ SAT Subject Tests	Yes	No	_____
❏ ACT	Yes	No	_____
❏ Placement Test	Yes	No	_____

Financial Aid Forms	Required		Date Completed
❏ FAFSA (January 1st)	Yes		_____
❏ CSS Financial Aid Profile	Yes	No	_____
❏ School forms	Yes	No	_____

Transcripts & Recommendations	Date Sent
❏ Transcripts sent	_____
❏ Recommendations sent	_____

Other Information Required?

School

❏ Reach ❏ Mid-Range ❏ Safety

School Name: _____

Contact: _____ **Telephone:** _____

Application Deadline: _____

Admission Interview? Yes No **Date scheduled:** _____

Portfolio required? Yes No **Requirements:** _____

Open House or College Tour/Visit Date: _____

Application type (check one)	Date sent	Method
❏ School Specific Application Form:	_____	Hard copy mailed
	_____	Online submission
or		
❏ Common Application:	_____	Hard copy mailed
	_____	Online submission
❏ Common Application Supplement:	_____	

Standardized Test Scores	Required		Date Taken
❏ SAT Reasoning Test	Yes	No	_____
❏ SAT Subject Tests	Yes	No	_____
❏ ACT	Yes	No	_____
❏ Placement Test	Yes	No	_____

Financial Aid Forms	Required		Date Completed
❏ FAFSA (January 1st)	Yes		_____
❏ CSS Financial Aid Profile	Yes	No	_____
❏ School forms	Yes	No	_____

Transcripts & Recommendations	Date Sent
❏ Transcripts sent	_____
❏ Recommendations sent	_____

Other Information Required?

School   ❏ Reach ❏ Mid-Range ❏ Safety

School Name: _____

Contact: _____ **Telephone:** _____

Application Deadline:_____

Admission Interview?   Yes   No   **Date scheduled:** _____

Portfolio required?   Yes   No   **Requirements:** _____

Open House or College Tour/Visit Date: _____

Application type (check one)	Date sent	Method
❏ School Specific Application Form:	_____ _____	Hard copy mailed Online submission
or		
❏ Common Application:	_____ _____	Hard copy mailed Online submission
❏ Common Application Supplement:	_____	

Standardized Test Scores	Required		Date Taken
❏ SAT Reasoning Test	Yes	No	_____
❏ SAT Subject Tests	Yes	No	_____
❏ ACT	Yes	No	_____
❏ Placement Test	Yes	No	_____

Financial Aid Forms	Required		Date Completed
❏ FAFSA (January 1st)	Yes		_____
❏ CSS Financial Aid Profile	Yes	No	_____
❏ School forms	Yes	No	_____

Transcripts & Recommendations	Date Sent
❏ Transcripts sent	_____
❏ Recommendations sent	_____

Other Information Required?

School   ❏ Reach ❏ Mid-Range ❏ Safety

School Name: _____

Contact: _____ **Telephone:** _____

Application Deadline: _____

Admission Interview? Yes No   **Date scheduled:** _____

Portfolio required? Yes No   **Requirements:** _____

Open House or College Tour/Visit Date: _____

Application type (check one)	Date sent	Method
❏ School Specific Application Form:	_____	Hard copy mailed
	_____	Online submission
or		
❏ Common Application:	_____	Hard copy mailed
	_____	Online submission
❏ Common Application Supplement:	_____	

Standardized Test Scores	Required		Date Taken
❏ SAT Reasoning Test	Yes	No	_____
❏ SAT Subject Tests	Yes	No	_____
❏ ACT	Yes	No	_____
❏ Placement Test	Yes	No	_____

Financial Aid Forms	Required		Date Completed
❏ FAFSA (January 1st)	Yes		_____
❏ CSS Financial Aid Profile	Yes	No	_____
❏ School forms	Yes	No	_____

Transcripts & Recommendations	Date Sent
❏ Transcripts sent	_____
❏ Recommendations sent	_____

Other Information Required?

School
❏ Reach ❏ Mid-Range ❏ Safety

School Name: _____

Contact: _____ **Telephone:** _____

Application Deadline: _____

Admission Interview? Yes No   **Date scheduled**: _____

Portfolio required? Yes No   **Requirements**: _____

Open House or College Tour/Visit Date: _____

Application type (check one)	Date sent	Method
❏ School Specific Application Form:	_____	Hard copy mailed
	_____	Online submission
or		
❏ Common Application:	_____	Hard copy mailed
	_____	Online submission
❏ Common Application Supplement:	_____	

Standardized Test Scores	Required		Date Taken
❏ SAT Reasoning Test	Yes	No	_____
❏ SAT Subject Tests	Yes	No	_____
❏ ACT	Yes	No	_____
❏ Placement Test	Yes	No	_____

Financial Aid Forms	Required		Date Completed
❏ FAFSA (January 1st)	Yes		_____
❏ CSS Financial Aid Profile	Yes	No	_____
❏ School forms	Yes	No	_____

Transcripts & Recommendations	Date Sent
❏ Transcripts sent	_____
❏ Recommendations sent	_____

Other Information Required?

School   ❏ Reach ❏ Mid-Range ❏ Safety

School Name: _____

Contact: _____ **Telephone:** _____

Application Deadline: _____

Admission Interview? Yes No   **Date scheduled:** _____

Portfolio required? Yes No   **Requirements:** _____

Open House or College Tour/Visit Date: _____

Application type (check one)	Date sent	Method
❏ School Specific Application Form:	_____	Hard copy mailed
	_____	Online submission
or		
❏ Common Application:	_____	Hard copy mailed
	_____	Online submission
❏ Common Application Supplement:	_____	

Standardized Test Scores	Required		Date Taken
❏ SAT Reasoning Test	Yes	No	_____
❏ SAT Subject Tests	Yes	No	_____
❏ ACT	Yes	No	_____
❏ Placement Test	Yes	No	_____

Financial Aid Forms	Required		Date Completed
❏ FAFSA (January 1st)	Yes		_____
❏ CSS Financial Aid Profile	Yes	No	_____
❏ School forms	Yes	No	_____

Transcripts & Recommendations	Date Sent
❏ Transcripts sent	_____
❏ Recommendations sent	_____

Other Information Required?

School

❏ Reach ❏ Mid-Range ❏ Safety

School Name: _____

Contact: _____ **Telephone:** _____

Application Deadline:_____

Admission Interview? Yes No **Date scheduled:** _____

Portfolio required? Yes No **Requirements:** _____

Open House or College Tour/Visit Date: _____

Application type (check one)	Date sent	Method
❏ School Specific Application Form:	_____ _____	Hard copy mailed Online submission
or		
❏ Common Application:	_____ _____	Hard copy mailed Online submission
❏ Common Application Supplement:	_____	

Standardized Test Scores	Required		Date Taken
❏ SAT Reasoning Test	Yes	No	_____
❏ SAT Subject Tests	Yes	No	_____
❏ ACT	Yes	No	_____
❏ Placement Test	Yes	No	_____

Financial Aid Forms	Required		Date Completed
❏ FAFSA (January 1st)	Yes		_____
❏ CSS Financial Aid Profile	Yes	No	_____
❏ School forms	Yes	No	_____

Transcripts & Recommendations	Date Sent
❏ Transcripts sent	_____
❏ Recommendations sent	_____

Other Information Required?

School   ❏ Reach   ❏ Mid-Range   ❏ Safety

School Name: _____

Contact: _____ **Telephone:** _____

Application Deadline: _____

Admission Interview?   Yes   No   **Date scheduled**: _____

Portfolio required?   Yes   No   **Requirements**: _____

Open House or College Tour/Visit Date: _____

Application type (check one)	Date sent	Method
❏ School Specific Application Form:	_____	Hard copy mailed
	_____	Online submission
or		
❏ Common Application:	_____	Hard copy mailed
	_____	Online submission
❏ Common Application Supplement:	_____	

Standardized Test Scores	Required		Date Taken
❏ SAT Reasoning Test	Yes	No	_____
❏ SAT Subject Tests	Yes	No	_____
❏ ACT	Yes	No	_____
❏ Placement Test	Yes	No	_____

Financial Aid Forms	Required		Date Completed
❏ FAFSA (January 1st)	Yes		_____
❏ CSS Financial Aid Profile	Yes	No	_____
❏ School forms	Yes	No	_____

Transcripts & Recommendations	Date Sent
❏ Transcripts sent	_____
❏ Recommendations sent	_____

Other Information Required?

School   ❏ Reach   ❏ Mid-Range   ❏ Safety

School Name: _____

Contact: _____ **Telephone:** _____

Application Deadline: _____

Admission Interview?   Yes   No   **Date scheduled:** _____

Portfolio required?   Yes   No   **Requirements:** _____

Open House or College Tour/Visit Date: _____

Application type (check one)	**Date sent**	**Method**
❏ School Specific Application Form:	_____	Hard copy mailed
	_____	Online submission
or		
❏ Common Application:	_____	Hard copy mailed
	_____	Online submission
❏ Common Application Supplement:	_____	

Standardized Test Scores	**Required**		**Date Taken**
❏ SAT Reasoning Test	Yes	No	_____
❏ SAT Subject Tests	Yes	No	_____
❏ ACT	Yes	No	_____
❏ Placement Test	Yes	No	_____

Financial Aid Forms	**Required**		**Date Completed**
❏ FAFSA (January 1st)	Yes		_____
❏ CSS Financial Aid Profile	Yes	No	_____
❏ School forms	Yes	No	_____

Transcripts & Recommendations	**Date Sent**
❏ Transcripts sent	_____
❏ Recommendations sent	_____

Other Information Required?

Writing Your College Essay

So, you have your college applications and are starting to fill them out. Your parents (who now observe you working diligently on your college applications) are no longer bugging you . . . and then you get to that one particular section. Dare we say it - **The College Essay!**

Relax, it is not as difficult as you think. You may not realize that the college essay is an excellent opportunity for you to let the college admissions office learn more information about that important applicant . . . YOU! In addition to learning more about you through your essay, the admissions office can better evaluate your communication and writing skills. That is why it is important to do your best when writing the essay. Your essay tells more about your thoughts and feelings, creativity and imagination. So, use the essay as a way to share your accomplishments (personal, community service, academic, athletic) but also to express interesting thoughts, or perhaps describe a challenge that you have overcome.

What Should You Write About? Very often, schools will either give you a topic to write about or ask you to write about one or more specific topics. Sometimes you are able to choose from a few options. Some colleges might allow you the freedom of writing about whatever you wish – you can choose a topic that interests you. *Remember, it is easier to write about something in which you are interested.* So select a topic that interests you and write specifically about it. Be careful not to go off on tangents – pick a topic and stick with it! Be creative so that your writing illustrates your thoughts to the reader. Give as much information as you can about yourself without going overboard (or the reader may get over-bored). Since the essay gives admissions important information about you, feel free to let loose and be creative. At the same time, if you are writing about yourself, remember that your writing should convey information about you as a person, such as personal qualities and character (note to self: do not exaggerate!).

Be Your Unique Self. The college essay is a great vehicle for your individuality and creativity, so do not be afraid to take chances. If you have the freedom to choose a topic, write about something a little different. One of our readers wrote about a soda can – his essay was an incredibly unique perspective on what is usually a not-so-interesting item. He made this unique topic appealing through his creativity – and to an admissions officer who is reading essays for hours at a time, this offbeat approach made his application stand out. Find your own voice and style that will show rather than tell.

Ready, Set, Write! Be sure to spend some time planning your ideas and thoughts in advance. Create an outline so your essay will progress smoothly from one thought to another. Remember to stick to your topic. Write within your comfort zone, in a consistent style, and consider your purpose and your audience. Be creative and flexible - remember to write about things that interest you. Be brief and to your point, then move on to your next thought or idea.

No Need to Get it "Write" the First Time. OK, you have completed your first draft – but do not be too hard on yourself – there will be a few other drafts to follow. After you have completed your first draft, let someone read it for you (English teacher or school counselor), then set it aside for a day or so. Pick it up again and then proofread and make changes. Be sure you are using a consistent style, appropriate spelling and grammar.

And In Conclusion...
Take advantage of the opportunity to use the college essay to give admissions more information about you. Your essay may be one of the more important elements used to make an admission decision, so put the time and energy into creating an excellent essay.

Summary

How to write an excellent essay:

- Select a topic that interests you and write specifically about it.

- Use the essay to give more information about you.

- Be yourself – use the essay to show your individuality and creativity.

- Create an outline so your essay will progress smoothly and stick to your topic.

- Write and review at least 3 drafts. Ask others to offer feedback.

- Be consistent in your style.

The Admissions Interview

Some colleges require an interview as part of the admissions process and others may only recommend an interview. If an interview is recommended, by all means have an interview! This will give the admissions committee a better look at who you are beyond test scores and grades. Interview times fill up quickly, so make your appointments early in the year. Contact the admissions office in September or October to set up an appointment for your interview. Before you go, prepare yourself well. Here are a few suggestions that may help:

Prepare for Your Interview
Yes, it is important to go prepared, but do not sound overly rehearsed. Go with an idea of what may be asked of you, but be yourself. Relax. The interviewer knows that you might be a little nervous.

Dress for Your Success
You probably do not need a suit and tie, but do dress "neat" casual. Do **not** wear jeans or shorts, sneakers, or a hat.

Do Your Homework
Though you do not need to know everything about the school, you should know at least something about it. Check the college's website before your interview. Websites offer a great deal of information and you might think of some new questions of your own.

What To Expect
Many questions you will encounter during your interviews will be similar from one school to the next. Remember that the admissions representative wants to know more about you than what is on your application or in your essay. Below are some questions you might be asked during the interview.

- Tell me about yourself and why you would like to attend our school.
- Tell me something you know about our school.
- Is there anything you would like to know about our school?
- In what ways do you plan to be part of the campus community?
- What hobbies and activities tell me most about you?
- Tell me about one of your achievements or learning experiences.
- Why do you want to major in _____?
- Tell me about your academic experience in high school.

Your Opportunity to Ask Questions

The Admissions Interview is also your opportunity to ask questions of the admissions representative. Bring your own questions to ask. It is okay to attend the interview with a list of questions.

After Your Interview

Send a thank you letter to the Admissions Office, even if you are no longer interested in the college. Courtesy, character and class go a long way. When you write your thank you letter, add something personal to the note, such as something you remembered from the interview.

Questions you might like to ask at your interview
Use lines below to write down a few questions of your own.

_____

_____

_____

_____

_____

_____

_____

_____

_____

_____

_____

Questions To Ask a College Admissions Counselor

Below is a list of questions to ask admissions representatives. If the admissions representative cannot answer your financial aid questions, then call or visit the Financial Aid Office at the school. Admissions reps and Financial Aid Officers want to answer your questions! So ask them.

- What are admissions deadlines?
- Do you require the SAT Reasoning Test, Subject Tests (which ones?) or the ACT?
- What types of student activities do you have on campus?
- What types of housing are available to freshmen?
- What is the average class size of freshmen classes?
- What is the student-to-faculty ratio?
- Can we visit the computer lab?
- Will I have the opportunity to study abroad? If so, where?
- How much is the Cost of Attendance (everything included)?
- What types of scholarships and financial aid are available to freshmen?
- What percentage of students receives financial aid?
- What is the median financial aid award for incoming freshmen?
- Are there any special scholarships available just for freshmen?
- Can freshmen bring their cars to campus?

College Athletics

So you want to play college athletics, but are not sure how to go about getting recruited. First, you should know that playing a sport in college is a whole different ball game than playing a sport in high school. Most college coaches will tell you that the biggest differences between high school and college athletics are the pace of the game and the time commitment. Are you willing to commit the time? Talk to some of your former high school teammates that are playing at the college level so you know what you can expect.

The Recruiting Process

The recruiting process is not easy. You have to work at it. Typically, schools are not going to come to you. You have to go to them. Here are some tips for getting recruited:

Start Early

It is difficult for coaches to recruit during their season, so start in the summer. If you can, gather your information and start contacting coaches during your junior year in high school. It pays to start early, especially if you are seeking an athletic scholarship.

NCAA Divisions

As you start your research, you will notice there are different divisions of college athletics: Divisions I, II and III. These divisions also are different in level of play but all are competing at a higher level than high school. To play a college sport at a Division I level, you have to be a stand out player. So be realistic about your talent and skills. In addition to Division I schools, it's a good idea to consider Divisions II and III schools as you may experience more playing time at these schools.

Scholarships

Only colleges in Divisions I and II offer athletic scholarships in specific sports. To qualify for a scholarship, you must complete the NCAA Eligibility Clearinghouse form. There is a cost to complete the form. Check with your high school athletic director to see if you qualify for a fee waiver. You can access and complete the NCAA Eligibility Clearinghouse form online at the NCAA Clearinghouse website at **<www.ncaaclearinghouse.net>**.

You can also find the paper version of the form in your athletic director's office or your school's guidance office. For more information about divisions and eligibility visit <**www.ncaa.org**>.

Contact college coaches

If you would like to ask questions about how colleges recruit athletes, you can e-mail, write a letter or call college coaches. Most telephone numbers and addresses for coaches can be found on a college's website. See the *Sample Letter* on page 44.

Put together an athletic resume

List all of your statistics from your sport and awards received. Do this the same way that you would list your academic accomplishments for the admissions office to read. See the *Athletic Resume Template* on page 45.

Send in a Videotape or DVD

Many proud family members and parents tape your performances in games. Make a tape or DVD of you playing your best and send them to coaches. Prior to sending, be absolutely sure that you properly label the tape or DVD with your name and telephone number. List your jersey number, position and team color on the label.

Some colleges may require a tape of specific skills. Every sport and school is different, so check with the college coach or department of athletics to find out exactly what is required.

No need to send a game tape of you having an "off" day. Send game tapes where your performance is successful. Most coaches prefer to see a full game on the tape, not just the highlights. Tape the entire game. Do not submit a tape where the camera only follows YOU around – coaches want to see an entire game to see how you play as part of your team.

Attend a Regional Showcase

Check with your high school coach or school's athletic director for more information about showcases. Many college coaches will attend these regional showcases to recruit students. There is sometimes a cost to participate.

Playing a Sport is a Serious Commitment

No matter what level you play, college athletics require a serious commitment, work ethic, good attitude, leadership skills and the ability to be a real team player. Part of the commitment might involve a great deal of travel, often requiring you to miss classes and complete homework on the road or in a hotel. Accepting a Division I or II athletic scholarship will require you to sign a contract with the school. To maintain your scholarship you may be required to meet certain criteria set by your coach. That may include pre-season and post-season workout sessions, extended or early practice hours (like 5:00 a.m. or 10:00 p.m.) curfews, and academic requirements, to mention a few.

Questions to Ask the College Coach
- What is your coaching style?
- How will I fit on your team?
- What is the time commitment to be part of your program? What time are practices? Do you have workout sessions for the pre-season?
- How does participation affect work in the classroom?
- How does this particular major affect my participation in your program?
- What is your philosophy on academics?
- What percentage of athletes at your school graduate in four years?
- What equipment is provided?

The following questions pertain to athletics in Divisions I and II:
- What is the process for the scholarship program?
- What is the length of the scholarship?
- What type of scholarship is it?
- If I am injured, how will this affect my scholarship?

Use the Sample Letter below to request more information from College Coaches

Sample Letter (or email) to A Coach

Date

Name of Coach
School Name
Address
City, State & Zip Code

Dear Coach _____,

I am a senior at **[Your High School]** *and participate on the school's* **[Your Sport]** *team as* **[Your Position].** *I would like to continue playing at the intercollegiate level. My plan is to visit your school in the next few weeks. Would you please send me information regarding your* **[Your Sport]** *program.*

If possible, I would like the opportunity to meet with you during my visit.

Enclosed [or "**Attached**" if an email] *please find my athletic resume and a copy of my next season's schedule. I look forward to meeting with you in the near future.*

Sincerely

Sign Your Letter

Your Name
Address
City, State and Zip Code
Telephone Number
E-mail Address

Use the template below to create your athletic resume.

Athletic Resume Template

Your Name
Address
City, State & Zip Code
Phone Number
E-mail address

Athletic Profile
In this section include your date of birth, height, weight, hand preference (left-handed or right-handed if this applies to your sport), position you play in your sport, the number of years you played varsity and other teams for which you participated. If you participate in track, include your events, times and distances.

Athletic Achievements
Include your statistics in your sport only for your high school years (do **not** include middle school statistics). This will vary from sport to sport (i.e. goals scored, assists, batting average, RBI's, running times, etc.). Include any high school awards you have received and records held (i.e. if you were elected captain or selected for all-state or all-star teams, etc.).

Academic
Include your graduation month and year, your cumulative high school grade point average (GPA), rank in class, and your SAT or ACT test scores.

References
List the name(s) and title(s) of your coach(es), mailing address, e-mail address and telephone number.

The SAT® & The ACT®

Getting Ready

You want to receive a high score on the SAT Reasoning Test or the ACT, right? Well, the best way to a good score is to prepare well.

First, you will need to know what test scores your colleges require for admission. Keep in mind that some schools do not require test scores. Some schools accept the ACT or SAT. Some highly selective colleges require one or more of the SAT Subject Tests. Be sure to find out what tests scores, if any, your schools require. Additionally, check all of your college admission application deadlines and decide the best date to take a test so that the scores arrive at your schools on time. It takes anywhere from 4 to 6 weeks for scores to be sent to colleges. If test scores are required by your schools, the scores are part of your application – so if they arrive late, you may not be considered for admission!

> **If your SAT or ACT scores are low** and your school(s) do not require the scores, do not submit them. Chances are, if you do submit them, they will be considered and could work against you.
>
> On the other hand, **if your scores are very good**, and your school does not require the scores, send them anyway! Putting your best foot forward cannot hurt in this case.
>
> Hint

Scholarships

Your test scores are not just used for college admissions. Some scholarship organizations use test scores as part of their requirements. Be sure to take the necessary test to be eligible.

Taking the Tests Again

If you have already taken the SAT or ACT and your test scores are a matter of concern, you may take the tests more than once. Almost everyone improves with good preparation. The key is to *prepare well*. So, register again and prepare yourself well. There is no substitute for studying. Your test scores will indicate how well you prepared.

Fee Waivers

Both the ACT and SAT cost money. Eligible students can receive fee waivers for either test. Ask your school counselor for a fee waiver or to find out if you qualify. Do not wait until the last minute! Fee waivers are not accepted for late SAT registrations.

How Colleges Use Test Scores

As you are about to learn, the ACT and SAT are different. But to colleges, your scores serve the same purpose – they provide more information about your skills and knowledge, and predict your success as a college student. Colleges that require test scores look at them carefully, sometimes putting too much emphasis on the score rather than the other qualities of a student. Participation in school activities, community service, a solid grade point average and a transcript that includes challenging classes ought to outweigh test scores, right? Hopefully. But keep in mind that some colleges are compared and ranked by the average test scores of incoming freshman – and since many colleges are concerned with competition and rankings, test scores can be an important factor. Recently, more and more colleges have decided against using test scores as part of the application process, but for the majority of schools, your score will be an important criterion for admission.

SAT or ACT?

Since the ACT is curriculum-based and assesses your subject knowledge (the stuff you learn in school, like English, math, science, etc.) and the SAT assesses critical thinking and problem solving skills, you may opt to take one rather than the other, assuming your schools accept either score. For example, if you are better at problem solving than quadratic formulae, then the SAT may be a better choice for you. So depending on your strengths and weaknesses, you may perform better on one test than the other. If you feel that is the case, it may be a good idea to take both exams. You may be more successful on one than the other and you can choose the higher score to send to colleges. Check with your schools prior to investing test fees and preparation time. They are offered on different Saturdays during the year and at different test sites. Check test registration deadlines to be sure you are not too late. Late fees are expensive!

Find out if your schools require the SAT Subject Tests!

SAT Subject Tests are 1 hour, multiple-choice tests. Subjects include *Literature, U.S. History, World History, Math Level 1, Math Level 2, Biology E/M (ecological or molecular), Chemistry, and Physics, and Language tests with listening.* Check the College Board website at <**www.collegeboard.com**> for more information about registration dates/instructions or to find out if your schools require Subject Tests.

So which test should you take?

To answer that question, let's learn a little more about the differences between the SAT Reasoning Test and the ACT Assessment.

The SAT Reasoning Test

You have probably heard about the SAT. Created by the College Board <**www.collegeboard.com**>, the SAT is a well-known college entrance exam used in many schools in the United States. The SAT measures critical thinking and deductive reasoning skills. It also tests ability to analyze and solve problems. The total testing time for the SAT is approximately 3 hours, 45 minutes.

What is on the Test?

There are three sections on the SAT - mathematics, critical reading and writing. There is an experimental section that is not scored. The experimental section is used to test new questions that may appear on future tests. Since you will not know which section is experimental, you should do your best in all sections.

How is the SAT scored?

All sections of the SAT are scored on a scale of 200-800; the writing section offers two sub-scores. The College Board sets the average for all test takers at 500 for each section. A perfect score on the SAT is 2400. What is a good score? Anywhere from 1400-1800 is average. A score of 2100 may be enough for most highly selective schools. School requirements will vary, so check with your schools regarding test score requirements. If you are not happy with your score, you can take the SAT Reasoning Test more than once. If you take the test more than once, your score report will contain all previous scores.

Does the SAT cost money?

Yes, the SAT costs money. The registration fee includes score reports sent to a specific number of colleges, but after that, you will have to pay for reports sent to additional schools. The College Board gives fee waivers to eligible students. Check with your school guidance office to find out if you qualify for a test fee waiver.

> **SAT REGISTRATION**
> Register for the
> SAT Reasoning Test
> and/or SAT Subject Tests
> at <**www.collegeboard.com**>

How to register for the SAT

If you complete the registration online <**www.collegeboard.com**> you can access your scores online 2 to 3 weeks after you have taken the test. There is no fee to view your scores online. If you register by paper form, your scores will be sent to you 4 to 6 weeks after the test date. Paper registration forms are available in your school guidance office.

What is on the SAT Reasoning Test?

Writing

Time: Total testing time is 60 minutes.
             One 35-minute multiple choice and one 25-minute essay.

Content: Multiple choice – identifying grammatical errors,
             improving sentences and paragraphs.

             Essay – ability to effectively communicate and support a
             viewpoint.

Score: Writing (WR) 200-800
             Multiple choice subscore: 20-80
             Essay subscore: 2 - 12

Critical Reading

Time: Total testing time is 70 minutes.
             Two 25-minute sections and one 20-minute section.

Content: Tests vocabulary in context, reasoning skills and reading
             comprehension.

             The tests consists of sentence completions and passage-
             based reading.

Score: Critical Reading (CR) 200-800

Mathematics

Time: Total testing time is 70 minutes.
             Two 25-minute sections and one 20-minute section.

Content: Tests number and operations, algebra I, II, geometry,
             statistics, probability and data analysis.

             The test consists of multiple choice items and student-
             produced responses.

Score: Mathematics (M) 200-800

ACT Assessment (ACT)

The ACT <**www.act.org**> is a curriculum-based entrance exam that measures your knowledge in English, mathematics, reading and science. The ACT has an optional writing test. The ACT is accepted at most colleges in the United States. The test assesses your overall educational development and, like the SAT, assesses your ability to complete college-level work.

The total testing time for the ACT is approximately 3 hours. Taking the writing test will add 30 minutes to the total time of the test. You can take the ACT more than once. Each time you take the test, your scores are reported separately, so you can choose what scores you would like to send to a college.

What is on the ACT?

The ACT has four sections: English, mathematics (up to trigonometry), reading, science, and an optional writing test.

How is the ACT scored?

There is a separate score for each section on the ACT. Each section is scored on a scale of 1 to 36 points, however, you will receive 12 separate scores on the ACT: 1 composite, 4 subject scores, and 7 sub-scores. The composite score is the most important. It is the average of the four subject scores. An average ACT composite score is between 17 and 23.

Does the ACT cost money?

Yes, the ACT costs money. There is a cost for registration. Like the SAT, the registration fee usually includes score reports sent to a specific number of colleges, but after that, you will have to pay for any reports sent to additional schools. The ACT has test fee waivers available to eligible students. Check with your guidance office to ask if you qualify for a fee waiver.

How to register for the ACT

You should register 4 to 5 weeks prior to your preferred test date. Students can choose to register online or by paper form for the ACT

> **ACT REGISTRATION**
> Register for the ACT
> at <**www.actstudent.org**>

Assessment or the ACT Assessment Plus (which includes the writing test). Your scores will be available to view online 2 to 3 weeks after the test date. Paper copies of score reports are sent to your home anywhere from 4 to 6 weeks after you take the test. And if you complete the writing test, your score report will be mailed to you after your writing scores are available.

What is on the ACT?

English
75 questions, 45 minutes

Content
Usage/Mechanics
Punctuation
Basic Grammar & Usage
Sentence Structure

Rhetorical Skills
Strategy
Organization
Style

Mathematics
60 questions, 60 minutes

Content
Pre-Algebra
Elementary Algebra
Intermediate Algebra
Coordinate Geometry
Plane Geometry
Trigonometry

Reading
40 questions, 35 minutes

Content
Prose Fiction
Humanities
Social Studies
Natural Sciences

Science
40 questions, 35 minutes

Content
Biology
Chemistry
Physics

(Earth Science/Physical Science
and Biology)

Writing Test (optional)

The Writing Test is a 30-minute essay that measures the student's writing skills. Students take a position on an issue from the writing prompt.

SAT and ACT Registration

Both the College Board and ACT send registration booklets to high schools. These are available at your high school guidance office. However, we recommend registering online – *the registration process is quicker when completed online* and if you are registering at the last minute, you will be able to complete the registration on time.

Register for the SAT at <**www.collegeboard.com**>

Register for the ACT at <**www.actstudent.org**>

Test Preparation Resources

Remember to prepare yourself well for the test. If you can afford to take a study or prep course (online or in a classroom) be sure to enroll weeks in advance of the test date so that you can prepare and avoid a last minute cramming session. Test preparation courses are helpful, but they can be expensive.

Free Test Prep Websites

There are many excellent **free** websites that can help prep you for the SAT or ACT. Here are three popular sites:

<www.number2.com>
<www.4tests.com>
<www.testprepreview.com>

Test Prep Books

There are also many test prep books that you can purchase to help you prepare for either test. Here are two test prep books recommended by our readers.

The Real ACT Prep Guide: The Only Official Prep Guide From The Makers Of The ACT by ACT Staff - available at <**www.act.org**>

The Official SAT Study Guide: For the New SAT
by College Board - available at <**www.collegeboard.com**>

Paying for College

Paying for college does not have to be difficult

By deciding to attend college, you have made an important decision that will help you reach your career and life goals. Achieving your college dreams will also require getting the money you need to see you through two to four years of school maybe more for certain professional careers.

The Cost of College

College Financial Aid Offices use the total cost of attending the college when they figure your financial aid package. The total **Cost of Attendance (COA)** for a college includes the following expenses:

- Tuition and Fees
- Room & Board
- Books & Supplies
- Transportation
- Personal Expenses (i.e. toiletries, clothing, etc.)

The **Cost of Attendance** at a school typically increases each year, so it is always best to call the school's Financial Aid Office or check the school's website for the most recent or up-to-date figures. As you consider the cost of college and how much you can contribute to your education, you should count on paying more money "out of your pocket" as prices increase each year.

Merit-Based and Need-Based Financial Aid

Financial aid is usually classified into two types. Each classification is based on the criteria through which the financial aid is awarded – either **merit-based** or **need-based. Merit-based** aid includes academic, athletic or other activity-type (i.e. musical instrument, special talents, etc.) scholarships. This is how your excellent grades or remarkable talent can really pay off. **Need-based** aid is awarded only on the basis of the financial need of the student and their family and is based on your (and your family's) income and assets. When a college figures your financial aid package they may use a combination of both types of aid to help you attend a school. Both merit and need-based aid can be from a variety of sources such as federal, state, regional and private sources.

Gift Aid and Self-Help Aid

Gift Aid is any type of financial aid (merit or need-based) that does not have to be repaid. Grants, scholarships do not have to be repaid. **Self-Help Aid** is financial aid that must be repaid, such as loans and the amount that a family is expected to contribute. The information you supply on your financial forms will determine whether or not you qualify for some financial aid programs. Colleges have limited financial aid and have limits regarding how they distribute gift aid and self-help aid. That is why it is very important to submit your financial aid forms as soon as you can (the first week of January).

Should You Take Out a Loan?

That depends on your financial situation. Few students can afford to pay for college without education loans. Most students will find themselves with some debt after college. In fact, the average indebtedness of today's college graduate is about $24,000 (the average wages for a college grad are also higher!). In many cases, scholarships and grants will not cover the entire cost of a college education. With rising tuition costs, many students find that they must take out government or private education loans, but that is not necessarily bad. In fact, most of the federal education loan programs that you will read about later in this section offer better repayment plans and lower interest rates than most private bank or consumer loans, making federal loans an easier way to help finance your education. Some education loans even offer forgiveness for working in specific jobs, like nursing and education. Check with your lender or state higher education agency for more information about these types of loans.

Unlike grants, scholarships and work-study, education loans are forms of financial aid that *must* be repaid, with interest. Make no mistake, education loans, whether federal or private, are real loans. Loans are a serious financial obligation, so give a great deal of thought about the amount before you decide to take out a loan.

Don't Take the Bait – Shop Around

All colleges are educational institutions, but not all have your best educational interest in mind. It is up to you to ask questions to decide what is in your best interest - educationally and financially. Some colleges are for-profit businesses and are concerned with their "bottom line." And the "bottom line" is money, namely yours. Beware of institutions that promise automatic admission, a large amount of financial aid (mostly loans) or a large non-refundable deposit. Reputable schools will ask for deposits, however, the deposit is refundable to a certain date and the money is put toward the cost of attendance. Ask specific questions about financial aid such as "how do you determine financial aid awards?" Or "how much do you gap students?" (see p.

59 for the definition of "gap"). If you feel that your financial aid questions are not being answered directly, you should probably cross the school from your list. Some schools will give a good package the first year and then significantly decrease your financial aid for the second year even though your financial information may have remained much the same as the previous year. These schools "bait" students with good financial aid packages to encourage them to attend the first year, and then count on the student to pick up a much larger amount of the cost for the second and subsequent years.

Before you apply for admission, ask all of your schools about the continuity of financial aid for following year(s). A reputable school's Financial Aid Office will <u>never</u> hesitate to completely answer your questions!

Loan Payment Chart

Thinking about loans? The chart below estimates payments over a 10-year period using an interest repayment rate of 6.95%. Your interest repayment rate may decrease after refinancing and making payments on time.

Loan Amount	# of Payments	Monthly Payment	Total Interest Paid	Total Payment
$5,000	120	$57.67	$1,920.80	$6,920.80
$6,000	120	$69.20	$2,304.66	$8,304.66
$7,000	120	$80.73	$2,689.02	$9,689.02
$8,000	120	$92.28	$3,072.85	$11,072.85
$9,000	120	$103.81	$3,457.18	$12,457.18
$10,000	120	$115.34	$3,841.53	$13,841.53
$12,500	120	$144.18	$4801.68	$17,301.68
$15,000	120	$173.02	$5,761.77	$20,761.77
$17,500	120	$201.85	$6,722.49	$24,222.49
$20,000	120	$230.69	$7,682.54	$27,682.54
$25,000	120	$288.36	$9,603.35	$34,603.35
$30,000	120	$346.03	$11,524.14	$41,524.14
$35,000	120	$403.71	$13,444.45	$48,444.45
$40,000	120	$461.38	$15,365.14	$55,365.14
$45,000	120	$519.04	$17,285.96	$62,285.96
$50,000	120	$576.72	$19,206.70	$69,206.70

Federal Perkins Loan Payment Chart

The chart below estimates payments over a 10-year period using the Perkins Loan fixed interest rate of 5%.

Loan Amount	# of Payments	Monthly Payment	Total Interest Paid	Total Payment
$4,000	120	$42.43	$1,091.14	$5,091.14
$6,000	120	$63.64	$1,636.72	$7,636.72
$8,000	120	$84.85	$2,182.29	$10,182.29
$10,000	120	$106.07	$2,727.86	$12,727.86
$12,000	120	$127.08	$3,273.43	$15,273.43
$14,000	120	$148.49	$3,819.01	$17,819.01
$16,000	120	$169.70	$4,364.58	$20,364.58
$18,000	120	$190.92	$4,910.15	$22,910.15
$20,000	120	$212.13	$5,455.72	$25,455.72

Plan to Help Pay for Your Education

College costs money, and you and your parents should expect to contribute to your educational investment. How much money will you have to contribute? This is determined in part by the **Free Application for Federal Student Aid (FAFSA)** and the schools to which you apply.

To be eligible for Federal Financial Aid, all students and parents (if you are a dependent student) must complete the FAFSA. With the exception of unsubsidized Stafford Loans and Parent Loans for Undergraduate Students (PLUS), Federal Financial Aid is need-based. You submit the FAFSA after January 1st and before June 30th. We recommend that you complete the FAFSA as soon as you can after January 1st. Some of your schools may also require you to complete the CSS/Financial Aid PROFILE® (see p. 76), but ALL schools that participate in Federal Financial Aid programs require the FAFSA. Additionally, most colleges have their own forms for you to complete. So you may have more than 3 different financial aid forms. Meeting deadlines is very important! You should submit the FAFSA even if you do not think you will qualify for any Federal Financial Aid. Sometimes being rejected for federal aid is necessary for receiving other financial aid such as scholarships or grants.

> **Hint**
>
> ### Are You a Dependent Student?
>
> Students under 24 years of age are dependent on their parents by federal law even if they do not live with their parents. If parents do not provide financial information on the FAFSA, a dependent student may not be considered for aid. So, if you are under 24, single, not a parent who provides more than 50% of financial care to your child, not a veteran, and not an orphan or ward of the state, you must include parental information on your FAFSA.
>
> If you are unable to get parent information, call your schools to let them know. They may be able to help.

Your Financial Aid Package Will Change Each Year

If you want to be considered for financial aid for each year you attend college, you must renew your **FAFSA** each year.   You will receive **FAFSA** renewal information in December or January. Keep in mind that the amount of your loans and cost of attendance will increase each year, based on your EFC, Federal Financial Aid programs, and your financial situation. Plan your budget carefully so that increases are not a surprise.

Are You Eligible for Federal Financial Aid?

For you to be eligible for Federal Financial Aid, you must meet the following criteria:

- Have a financial need.
- Be a United States citizen or an eligible non-citizen.
- Have a valid Social Security Number.
- If you are male, you must register for the selective service.
- Be enrolled in an eligible diploma, certificate, associate, bachelor, or graduate degree program.
- Maintain satisfactory academic progress once in college.

Your Expected Family Contribution (EFC)

Once you submit your FAFSA, you will receive a **Student Aid Report (SAR).** In the top right corner of the SAR, you will see your Expected Family Contribution or **EFC** (*circled on the sample SAR below*). This is the amount you and your family are expected to contribute to your education for one year.

UNITED STATES DEPARTMENT OF EDUCATION

1-800-4-FED-AID (1-800-433-3243 or TTY: 1-800-730-8913)

We Help Put America Through School

www.fafsa.ed.gov

000117C041

CHRISTOPER E. STUDENT
1234 ABCDEFGHIJKLMNOPQRSTUVWXYZABCD
ABCDEFGHIJKLMNOPQ, MD 12345

EFC: 00000

Dear

Thank you for submitting your information for federal student aid to the U.S. Department of Education.

This is your Student Aid Report (SAR) for the **2004-2005** award year. Keep a copy of this SAR for your records.

You (the Student)

Here is where you are this year in the process of applying for student financial aid:

1. You applied for financial aid by completing a Free Application for Federal Student Aid (FAFSA).

2. **Now you should check your SAR information. If it is correct, you do not need to return it to us.**

3. Your school has the authority to request copies of certain financial documents to verify information you reported on your application.

How Is My EFC Determined?

The EFC amount is based on you and your family's earnings, assets, family size and number of students in your family who are attending college. Remember, you will complete the FAFSA to determine how much you and your family can afford to pay for one year <u>and</u> to qualify for Federal Financial Aid programs. The EFC does NOT indicate how much financial aid you will receive from colleges. Unfortunately, colleges DO NOT have to meet your financial need! Your **financial need** is determined by subtracting your EFC from the school's cost of attendance as in the example below:

Cost of Attendance	$15,000
- EFC	$ 4,000
Financial Need =	**$11,000**

What is a Gap?

A student is fully funded by a college when the total sum of the financial aid package covers 100% of a student's <u>financial need</u>. Few schools will fully fund a student's education. To meet the student's financial need in the previous example, a college would have to offer $11,000 in the financial aid package. That is the good news. But many schools will "gap" students, meaning that the total amount of grants, scholarships, loans and work-study awarded does not cover the full cost of a student's financial need. Instead, the student is left with an amount of the college cost called the unmet need or a "gap." For students depending on aid, a gap can create a problem. We will discuss other ways to handle unmet need later. Be sure to do your research with the school's Financial Aid Office before you apply for admission. Find out if they gap all students or if financial need is fully covered. A large amount of unmet need is an unwelcome surprise in March and may keep you from attending the school.

Here is an example of a gap using the financial need from the previous page.

Cost of Attendance	$15,000
- EFC	$ 4,000
Financial Need =	**$11,000**

Let's say that a college's financial aid package awarded to you is $9,000 (including gift and self-help aid). To find the gap, simply subtract the total financial aid package from the financial need. The result is the gap or unmet need.

Cost of Attendance	$15,000
- EFC	$ 4,000
Financial Need =	$11,000
- Financial Aid Package	$ 9,000
GAP(unmet need) =	**$ 2,000**

Special Circumstances

Although the formula used to determine eligibility for Federal Financial Aid is basically the same for all applicants, there is some flexibility for special circumstances. For example, the Financial Aid Administrator may adjust the Cost of Attendance or the information used to calculate the EFC to account for special circumstances a family may encounter. Such special circumstances may include unemployment, unusually high medical expenses, etc. You will, of course, have to provide documentation to support your information. The Financial Aid Administrator will decide whether or not special circumstances will impact a financial aid package. The decision is final and cannot be appealed.

Start your Scholarship Search Early

To be sure you are considered for as much gift aid as possible, start your scholarship search early. It is never too early to start your scholarship search.

Scholarships fall into these main categories:
1. Local
2. Institutional (the colleges)
3. State
4. Regional
5. National

You have a better chance of receiving local scholarships because of smaller applicant pools. Local scholarships available through your school or community organizations have a smaller amount of applicants than most national, regional and state scholarships. The more applicants the less likely your chances are to receive a scholarship. Since national, regional and state level scholarships are open to a larger population of students, they attract more applicants. But even though your odds might not be as good as local scholarships, you should still apply, because there is one guarantee: You will not receive a scholarship if you do not apply.

There are many online sites where you can search for scholarships. Check out these free sites to start your scholarship search: <**www.fastweb.com**> and <**www.theoldschool.org**>. Remember that these sites will not contain your local area scholarships and are not the only places you should search for scholarships. For information on local scholarships that may be available to you, contact your high school guidance office or state higher education agency.

How Private Scholarships Can Affect Your Financial Aid Award

The amount of scholarships you receive from private sources (i.e. local, state, regional, national) may affect your financial aid award differently at each college. For example, if you receive a $500 local scholarship, you must report the scholarship to your colleges. This may (or may not) change your financial aid award. Some schools use private scholarships to fill unmet need. Some schools will lower loan awards (if any). For example, if your financial aid award from a school includes a loan of $2,000, the loan amount may change to $1,500 to account for the additional $500 you received from a private scholarship. Some schools may lower the amount of self-help aid, and some may lower gift aid. Contact the institution to determine if and how your financial aid package will be affected by private scholarships.

About Scholarship Scams

Many students and their families become easy targets for scholarship scams. Sometimes you will see these scholarships advertised via email, campus newspapers, flyers, or regular mail. Never send money to apply for a scholarship.

There are many free resources for scholarships available in your guidance office or online. Sad to say, but some companies offer these free lists at a cost to applicants. Do not pay for free information. Check with your school guidance office before you decide to pay someone to do the work for you. Do not buy the sales pitch. Only you can apply for your scholarships. *Remember:* No one can guarantee you a grant or scholarship. No one. For more information on how to recognize or report a scholarship scam, contact:

The National Fraud
Information Center
1-800-876-7060

Reserve Officer Training Corps (ROTC) Scholarships

If you are interested attending college and serving in the military, ROTC programs are a great way to pay for college. Army, Marine Corps, Navy, and the Air Force ROTC programs are available in over 1,000 schools throughout the United States. Students completing ROTC programs become officers in those services upon graduation. ROTC scholarships are competitive and are awarded on merit. The length, amount, and terms of scholarships are different in each service. All services offer up to four-year scholarships that may include full tuition, books, fees, and a monthly stipend. Some services offer health-related or nurse ROTC programs. When applying for a scholarship, ROTC admissions representatives will consider a student's high school academic record, test scores, extracurricular activities, the admissions interview as well as other criteria determined by each program, including passing a physical exam and physical assessments.

For more information visit **<www.rotc.org>** or the following service-specific websites:

Air Force ROTC **<www.afrotc.com>**
Army ROTC **<www.goarmy.com/rotc>**
Navy ROTC **<www.nrotc.navy.mil>**
Marine ROTC **<www.marines.com>**

KEEPING TRACK OF YOUR SCHOLARSHIPS

Put time and energy into applying for scholarships available from local sources (see your school counselor), colleges to which you are applying, and through the internet – it can really pay off. Local scholarships are always your best bet! All scholarships have deadlines and some may have additional requirements. If you miss a deadline or forget to send the requirements, your scholarship application will be denied. Keep track of these important details by using this form. Good Luck!

	Scholarship	Amount	Application	Deadline	Essay	Transcript	Letter of Recomm.	Portfolio Other
	The Robinson Foundation Scholarship Award	*$500*	*done*	*10/21*	*done*	*sent 10/15*	*yes*	*n/a*
1								
2								
3								
4								
5								
6								
7								
8								
9								
10								
11								
12								
13								
14								
15								
16								
17								
18								
19								
20								
21								
22								

Types of Financial Aid

As you read earlier, not all colleges are going to meet your financial need. Additionally, when colleges send you an award package, it might not necessarily be a "good" package. Whether or not a package is good depends on your financial situation, but a good package (for a student who needs financial aid to attend a college) will include at least 60% **Gift Aid**. Take a look at the following types of financial aid. You will discover that there are many options available to help pay for college expenses. If you have questions about types of financial aid, call the Financial Aid Office at any of the schools to which you are applying. Besides being experts, Financial Aid Officers are good people to know!

As you review the following information, you will notice that some of the aid has the word "federal" attached. These are all types of aid for which you may qualify when you complete the FAFSA. Here are some with which you are about to become a little more familiar:

Self-Help Aid
Financial aid that MUST be paid back
- Loans from private banks
- Loans from states, colleges & other institutions
- Federal Perkins Loans
- Federal Stafford Loans (unsubsidized & subsidized)

Gift Aid
Financial aid that does NOT have to be paid back
- Grants (state-sponsored)
- Federal Pell Grant
- Federal Supplemental Educational Opportunity Grant (FSEOG)
- Institutional grants & scholarships from the colleges
- Scholarships (Local, State, Regional, National)

Other Financial Aid
- Federal Work-Study
- Federal Parent Loans for Undergraduate Students (PLUS)
- State/Regional Tuition Programs
  (check with your colleges or state higher education agency)

Federal Financial Aid Programs

The FAFSA allows qualified students access to many Federal Financial Aid programs. To be considered for these programs, the student must file the FAFSA as early as possible after January 1st. Federal Financial Aid programs for which you may qualify include the following programs cited from the U.S. Department of Education's website <**www.studentaid.ed.gov**>.

Federal Pell Grant

Not all students will receive a Pell Grant, but if you are eligible the amount will range from $400 to $4,050 (most recent figures). How much you get depends on your Expected Family Contribution, cost of attendance, whether you are a full-time or part-time student, and whether you attend school for a full academic year or less.

Federal Supplemental Educational Opportunity Grant (FSEOG)

FSEOGs are awarded to undergraduate students with exceptional financial need. The amount of FSEOG funds received depends not only on your financial need but also on the amount of other aid you receive and the availability of funds at your school. Receiving other aid might reduce the amount of your FSEOG award. FSEOGs are administered by the Financial Aid Office at each of the schools participating in the program. The federal government provides a certain amount of FSEOG funds each year to participating schools. So, make sure you submit your FAFSA as early as possible to be considered for these funds. You can get between $100 and $4,000 a year, depending on when you apply, your financial need, the funding level of the school you are attending, and the school's Financial Aid Office policies.

Federal Work-Study

This federal program is called Federal Work-Study and is administered by schools participating in the program. This program allows students to work part-time while in school. Most Work-Study jobs are on campus. The government provides those schools with a certain amount of Work-Study funds each year, but when all funds have been awarded, no additional Work-Study awards can be made for that year. So, again, make sure you file your FAFSA as early as possible to be considered for these funds. Note: The student is responsible for finding Work-Study positions while at school. Students apply for Work-Study positions by applying directly to the campus office advertising the job.

Federal Perkins Loan

This is a low-interest loan that must be repaid. Perkins loans are for students with exceptional financial need. Federal Perkins Loans are dispersed through a college's Financial Aid Office. These loans can be up to $4,000 per year to a maximum of $20,000 for an undergraduate student (most recent figures).

Federal Stafford Loans

Federal Stafford loans are low-interest loans made to students attending college at least half-time. Loans are made by a bank, credit union, or savings and loan association. Like other loans, Stafford loans must be repaid. Your loan limits depend on what year you are in school (see p. 66), whether you are a dependent student, and whether you receive "subsidized" or "unsubsidized" Stafford Loans.

Subsidized Stafford Loan

If you demonstrate financial need, you can borrow a direct loan or a "subsidized" loan to cover some or all of your financial need. For a subsidized loan, the U.S. Department of Education pays the interest while you are in school at least half-time and during a period of approved deferment (a postponement of loan payments). The amount of your subsidized loan cannot exceed your financial need.

Unsubsidized Stafford Loan

You might be able to receive loan funds beyond your subsidized loan limit or even if you do not have demonstrated financial need. In that case, you would receive an unsubsidized loan. To determine the amount of your unsubsidized loan, your school will use this equation:

Cost of Attendance
- the Federal Pell Grant (if eligible)
- the Subsidized Stafford Loan (if eligible)
- any other financial aid you receive

———————————————————

= Amount of unsubsidized loan you can receive
  (up to annual maximum)

Note: For an unsubsidized loan, you are responsible for the interest from the time the loan is disbursed until it is paid in full (even when you are in school!). As interest accumulates, the total amount you repay will be higher than if you paid the interest all along.

Federal Parent Loan for Undergraduate Students (PLUS)

The PLUS enables a parent with a good credit history to borrow for each child who is enrolled at least half-time and is a dependent student. PLUS loans are made through the program mentioned above. Interest accrues immediately. Loans are made by a bank, credit union, or savings and loan association. Like other loans, the PLUS must be repaid.

FEDERAL FINANCIAL AID PROGRAMS
(Note: Amounts are subject to change)

AID PROGRAM	DESCRIPTION	ANNUAL AMOUNT	REPAYMENT
Federal Pell Grant	Grant aid for undergraduates. Eligibility based on financial need.	Up to $4,050	None
Federal Supplemental Educational Opportunity Grant (FSEOG)	Grant aid for undergraduates. Eligibility based on financial need. Priority given to students who qualify for Federal Pell Grants.	Up to $4,000	None
Federal Work-Study	Allows students to work part-time. The college coordinates the job. Eligibility is based on need. Priority given to applicants qualifying for Federal Pell Grants.	Varies	None
Federal Perkins Loan	A Federal Perkins Loan is a low-interest (5%) loan for students with exceptional financial need; made through a school's Financial Aid Office. The school is the lender, and the loan is made with government funds.	$100 to $4,000	Yes
Federal Stafford Loan (subsidized & unsubsidized)	If eligible for a subsidized loan, the government will pay interest while in school, for the first six months after you leave school. Dependent on financial need. *Loan limits increase each year - $2,625 first-year $3,500 second; $5,500 third & fourth years.	Up to $2,625*	Yes
Federal PLUS Loan (Parent Loan for Undergraduate Student)	Parents who have an acceptable credit history can borrow a PLUS Loan to pay the education expenses of a child who is a dependent student enrolled at least half-time in an eligible program at an eligible school. ** The yearly limit on a PLUS Loan is equal to the cost of attendance minus any other financial aid received. If the cost of attendance is $6,000, for example, and the student receives $4,000 in other financial aid, parents can borrow up to $2,000.	**	Yes

Hint

To download your free guide to Student Aid
visit <**www.studentaid.ed.gov**>

Not All Financial Aid Packages are Created Equal

Now that you understand a little more about financial aid and how colleges figure financial aid packages, the following pages will illustrate the difference between a good package and a weak package. A helpful guideline to follow: *A financial aid package that delivers at least 60% Gift Aid (of the student's financial need) is a pretty good package.* You will still need to take into consideration the Cost of Attendance and your EFC – and, of course, any unmet need.

Colleges come with different price tags so you will need to sharpen your pencil and compare financial aid packages when the time comes. Just because some institutions are more expensive than others does not mean you should not apply to them or that you will have to pay significantly more to attend. Do not let the price tag scare you!   Some of those higher priced institutions offer excellent financial aid packages with plenty of Gift Aid. Ask questions before you apply for admission. Below are some important questions you should ask the Financial Aid Office at each school. Keep in mind, answers may be quite different for each school!

Questions to Ask Financial Aid Officers

- Does your school meet 100% of a student's financial need?
- Do you gap your students? If so, by how much?
- What type of formula do you use when distributing financial aid? Need-based, merit-based or both?
- What financial aid forms do you require? When are they due?
- When can I expect to receive a financial aid package?
- Is there a commitment for financial aid beyond the first year?
- Does financial aid decrease for the second year? What can I expect?
- What type of grants, loans and scholarships does your college offer?
- How do outside scholarships affect my financial aid award? Are outside scholarships deducted from my loans, gift aid or unmet need?

What's a Good Package?
A financial aid package that delivers at least 60% gift aid toward the total financial need is considered a good financial aid package.

Hint

What's the Difference?

Now that you know more about financial aid and how it is packaged, let's take a closer look at the difference between good and weak financial aid packages.

A Good Financial Aid Package

The Cost of Attendance **(COA)** at
Sample College for one year: **$27,000**

Your Expected Family Contribution **(EFC)**
from the Student Aid Report: **$ 2,000**

Sample College has offered our student the following financial aid package:

Gift Aid		**Self-Help Aid**	
Federal Pell Grant	$ 3,000	Federal Stafford Loan	$2,625
Merit Scholar Award	$ 2,000	Federal Perkins Loan	$2,500
Presidential Scholarship	$11,000		
State Education Grant	$ 3,000		

*Now let's look at the total **financial aid package** from Sample:*

The Amount of **Gift Aid**:	$19,000
The Amount of **Self-Help Aid**:	$ 5,125
Total Financial Aid Award:	$24,125

*If you need financial aid to attend college, then you should consider any unmet need or gap. As you read earlier, many schools will "gap" students, meaning that the total amount of grants, scholarships, loans and work-study awarded does not cover the full cost of a student's financial need. Here's how **unmet need** is figured, based on the example above:*

Cost of Attendance **(COA)**	$27,000
- (minus) **EFC**	$ 2,000
Total **Financial Need**	$25,000
- Total **Award**	$24,125
= Total Unmet Need	$ 875

A Good Deal

What makes this a good package is not simply that the unmet need (or gap) is only $875, but also the total amount of Gift Aid is over 70% of the Total Financial Need. This a good deal for our student!

A Weak Financial Aid Package

The total Cost of Attendance (COA) at
Example University for one year: **$13,000**

Your Expected Family Contribution (EFC)
from the Student Aid Report: **$ 2,000**

Example University has offered our student the following financial aid package:

Gift Aid		Self-Help Aid	
Federal Pell Grant	$2,000	Federal Stafford Loan	$2,625
FSEOG	$1,000	Federal Perkins Loan	$2,000
Academic Merit Scholarship	$1,400		

*Now let's look at the total **financial aid package** from Example:*

The Amount of **Gift Aid**:	$ 4,400
The Amount of **Self-Help Aid**:	$ 4,625
Total Financial Aid Award:	$ 9,025

*If you need financial aid to attend college, then you should consider any unmet need or gap. Here's how the **unmet need** is figured based on the example above:*

Cost of Attendance **(COA)**	$13,000
- (minus) **EFC**	$ 2,000
Total **Financial Need**	$11,000
- Total **Award**	$ 9,025
= Total Unmet Need	**$ 1,975**

Could Be Better

The total unmet need or gap is $1,975 - which is a significant shortfall, considering the amount of loans awarded. Additionally, the gift aid represents only 40% of the Total Financial Need. Example University would need to sweeten this package with at least $3,000 more gift aid or our student might want to shop elsewhere (i.e. attend a college that offers a better financial aid package). Colleges package aid differently. This example demonstrates why you should consider admission and financial aid with <u>several colleges</u>. Besides, exploring a diversity of colleges allows you to choose the best school for you!

Not Eligible for Federal Aid?

Even if you are not eligible for federal aid, you might be eligible for financial assistance from your state. You can also check out state-specific tuition programs that may provide reduced tuition or reciprocity programs. Contact your state higher education agency for more information:

Alabama
Alabama Commission on Higher Education
P.O. Box 302000
Montgomery, AL 36130-2000
Phone: (334) 242-1998
Toll-Free: (800) 960-7773
Toll-Free Restrictions: AL residents only
www.ache.state.al.us

Alaska
Alaska Commission on
  Postsecondary Education
3030 Vintage Boulevard
Juneau, AK 99801-7100
Phone: (907) 465-2962
Toll-Free: (800) 441-2962
www.alaskaadvantage.state.ak.us

Arizona
Arizona Commission for
  Postsecondary Education
Suite 550
2020 North Central Avenue
Phoenix, AZ 85004-4503
Phone: (602) 258-2435
www.azhighered.gov

Arkansas
Arkansas Department of Higher Education
114 East Capitol
Little Rock, AR 72201-3818
Phone: (501) 371-2000
www.arkansashighered.com

California
California Student Aid Commission
P.O. Box 419027
Rancho Cordova, CA 95741-9027
Phone: (916) 526-7590
Toll-Free: (888) 224-7268
www.csac.ca.gov

Colorado
Colorado Commission on Higher Education
Suite 1200
1380 Lawrence Street
Denver, CO 80204
Phone: (303) 866-2723
www.state.co.us/cche_dir/hecche.html

Connecticut
Connecticut Department of Higher Education
61 Woodland Street
Hartford, CT 06105-2326
Phone: (860) 947-1800
Toll-Free: (800) 842-0229
www.ctdhe.org

Delaware
Delaware Higher Education Commission
Carvel State Office Building
820 North French Street
Wilmington, DE 19801
Phone: (302) 577-3240
Toll-Free: (800) 292-7935
www.doe.k12.de.us/high-ed

District of Columbia
State Education Office
441 Fourth Street, NW
Washington, DC 20001
Phone: (202) 727-2824
Toll-Free: (877) 485-6751
www.seo.dc.gov

Florida
Council for Education Policy
  Research & Improvement
111 West Madison Street
Suite 574 Pepper Building
Tallahassee, FL 32399-1400
Telephone: 850-488-7894

Georgia
Georgia Student Finance Commission
State Loans Division
2082 East Exchange Place, Suite 230
Tucker, GA 30084
Phone: (770) 724-9000
Toll-Free: (800) 505-4732
www.gsfc.org

Hawaii
Hawaii State Postsecondary
  Education Commission
Room 209
2444 Dole Street
Honolulu, HI 96822-2302
Phone: (808) 956-8213

Idaho
Idaho State Board of Education
P.O. Box 83720
Boise, ID 83720-0037
Phone: (208) 334-2270
www.boardofed.idaho.gov

Illinois
Illinois Student Assistance Commission
1755 Lake Cook Road
Deerfield, IL 60015-5209
Phone: (847) 948-8500
Toll-Free: (800) 899-4722

Indiana
State Student Assistance
    Commission of Indiana
Suite 500
150 West Market Street
Indianapolis, IN 46204-2811
Phone: (317) 232-2350
Toll-Free: (888) 528-4719
Toll-Free Restrictions: IN residents only
www.in.gov/ssaci

Iowa
Iowa College Student Aid Commission
Fourth Floor
200 10th Street
Des Moines, IA 50309
Phone: (515) 242-3344
Toll-Free: (800) 383-4222
www.iowacollegeaid.org

Kansas
Kansas Board of Regents
Curtis State Office Building
Suite 520
1000 SW Jackson Street
Topeka, KS 66612-1368
Phone: (785) 296-3421
www.kansasregents.org

Kentucky
Kentucky Higher Education
    Assistance Authority
P.O. Box 798
Frankfort, KY 40602-0798
Phone: (502) 696-7200
Toll-Free: (800) 928-8926
www.kheaa.com

Louisiana
Louisiana Office of Student
    Financial Assistance
P.O. Box 91202
Baton Rouge, LA 70821-9202
Phone: (225) 922-1012
Toll-Free: (800) 259-5626
www.osfa.state.la.us

Maine
Finance Authority of Maine
P.O. Box 949
Augusta, ME 04332-0949
Phone: (207) 623-3263 x313
Toll-Free: (800) 228-3734
www.famemaine.com

Maryland
Maryland Higher Education Commission
839 Bestgate Road, Suite 400
Annapolis, MD 21401-3013
Phone: (410) 260-4500
Toll-Free: (800) 974-1024
Toll-Free Restrictions: MD residents only
www.mhec.state.md.us

Massachusetts
Massachusetts Board of Higher Education
One Ashburton Place
Boston, MA 02108
Phone: (617) 994-6950
www.mass.edu/

Michigan
Michigan Higher Education
    Assistance Authority
Office of Scholarships and Grants
P.O. Box 30462
Lansing, MI 48909-7962
Phone: (517) 373-3394
Toll-Free: (888) 447-2687
www.michigan.gov/mistudentaid

Minnesota
Minnesota Office of Higher Education
1450 Energy Park Drive, Suite 350
Saint Paul, MN 55108-5227
Phone: (651) 642-0567
Toll-Free: (800) 657-3866

Mississippi
Mississippi Office of
    Student Financial Aid
3825 Ridgewood Road
Jackson, MS 39211-6453
Phone: (601) 432-6997
Toll-Free: (800) 327-2980
www.ihl.state.ms.us/financialaid

Missouri
Missouri Department of
    Higher Education
3515 Amazonas Drive
Jefferson City, MO 65109-5717
Phone: (573) 751-2361
Toll-Free: (800) 473-6757
www.dhe.mo.gov

VC LIBRARY

Montana
Montana Higher Education
  Student Assistance
Student Assistance Foundation
P.O. Box 5209
Helena, MT 59604-5209
Toll-free: (800) 852-2761
www.mhesac.org

Nebraska
Nebraska Coordinating Commission
  for Postsecondary Education
P.O. Box 95005
Lincoln, NE 68509-5005
Phone: (402) 471-2847
www.ccpe.state.ne.us

Nevada
University and Community College
  System of Nevada
System Administration North
2601 Enterprise Road
Reno, Nevada 89512
Telephone: 775-784-4905
http://system.nevada.edu

New Hampshire
New Hampshire Postsecondary
  Education Commission
3 Barrell Court , Suite 300
Concord, NH 03301-8543
Phone: (603) 271-2555
www.state.nh.us/postsecondary

New Jersey
Commission on Higher Education
20 West State Street
P.O. Box 542
Trenton, NJ 08625-0542
Phone: (609) 292-4310
www.state.nj.us/highereducation

Higher Education Student
  Assistance Authority
P.O. Box 540
Quakerbridge Plaza
Trenton, NJ 08625-0540
Phone: (609) 588-3226
Toll-Free: (800) 792-8670
www.hesaa.org

New Mexico
New Mexico Commission on
  Higher Education
1068 Cerrillos Road
Santa Fe, NM 87505
Phone: (505) 476-6500
Toll-Free: (800) 279-9777
www.hed.state.nm.us

New York
New York State Higher
  Education Services Corporation
99 Washington Avenue
Albany, NY 12255
Phone: (518) 473-1574
Toll-Free: (888) 697-4372
www.hesc.com

North Carolina
North Carolina State Education
  Assistance Authority
P.O. Box 13663
Research Triangle Park, NC 27709-3663
Phone: (919) 549-8614
Toll-Free: (866) 866-2362
www.ncseaa.edu

North Dakota
North Dakota Student Financial
  Assistance Program
600 East Boulevard Avenue
Bismarck, ND 58505-0230
Phone: (701) 328-4114

Ohio
Ohio Board of Regents
State Grants and Scholarships Dept.
57 East Main Street
Fourth Floor
Columbus, OH 43215
Phone: (614) 466-7420
Toll-Free: (877) 428-8246
www.regents.state.oh.us

Oklahoma
Oklahoma State Regents
  for Higher Education
655 Research Parkway
Oklahoma City, OK 73104
Phone: (405) 225-9100
Toll-Free: (800) 858-1840
www.okhighered.org

Oregon
Student Assistance Commission
1500 Valley River Drive
Eugene, OR 97401
Phone: (541) 687-7400
Toll-Free: (800) 452-8807
www.osac.state.or.us

Pennsylvania
Office of Postsecondary and
  Higher Education
Department of Education
333 Market Street
Harrisburg, PA 17126
Phone: (717) 787-5041
www.pdehighered.state.pa.us

VC LIBRARY

Rhode Island
Rhode Island Higher Education
  Assistance Authority
560 Jefferson Boulevard
Warwick, RI 02886
Phone: (401) 736-1100
www.riheaa.org

Rhode Island Office
  of Higher Education
301 Promenade Street
Providence, RI 02908-5748
Phone: (401) 222-6560
www.ribghe.org

South Carolina
South Carolina Commission
  on Higher Education
1333 Main Street, Suite 200
Columbia, SC 29201
Phone: (803) 737-2260
www.che400.state.sc.us

South Dakota
South Dakota Board of Regents
306 East Capitol Avenue
Pierre, SD 57501
Phone: (605) 773-3455
www.ris.sdbor.edu

Tennessee
Tennessee Higher
  Education Commission
404 James Robertson Parkway
Nashville, TN 37243-0830
Phone: (615) 741-3605
www.state.tn.us/thec

Texas
Texas Higher Education Coordinating Board
P.O. Box 12788
Austin, TX 78711
Phone: (512) 427-6101
www.thecb.state.tx.us

Utah
Utah State Board of Regents
60 South 400 West
Salt Lake City, UT 84101-1284
Phone: (801) 321-7103
www.utahsbr.edu

Vermont
Vermont Student Assistance Corp
Champlain Mill
1 Main Street, Third Floor
P.O. Box 2000
Winooski, VT 05404-2601
Phone: (802) 655-9602
Toll-Free: (800) 642-3177
www.vsac.org

Virginia
State Council of Higher Education
  for Virginia
James Monroe Building
101 North 14th Street, 9th floor
Richmond, VA 23219
Phone: (804) 225-2600
www.schev.edu

Washington
Higher Education Coordinating
  Board of Washington State
917 Lakeridge Way
Olympia, WA 98504-3430
Phone: (360) 753-7800
www.hecb.wa.gov

West Virginia
West Virginia Higher Education
  Policy Commission
1018 Kanawha Boulevard, East
Charleston, WV 25301
Phone: (304) 558-2101
www.hepc.wvnet.edu

Wisconsin
Wisconsin Higher Educational
  Aids Board
131 West Wilson Street
Madison, WI 53703
Phone: (608) 267-2206
http://heab.state.wi.us

Wyoming
Wyoming Community
  College Commission
2020 Carey Avenue
Cheyenne, WY 82002
Phone: (307) 777-7763
www.communitycolleges.wy.edu

Summary

- The Cost of Attendance (COA) is the total cost of attending a college, including tuition and fees, room and board, books and supplies, transportation, and personal expenses (i.e. toiletries, clothing, etc.).

- A financial aid "package" is a combination of different forms of Gift Aid and Self-Help Aid to help you attend a school. Gift Aid, such as grants and scholarships do not have to be repaid. Self-Help Aid can be loans and the amount that a family is expected to contribute.

- Plan to help pay for your education. How much money will you have to contribute? This is determined in part by the Free Application for Federal Student Aid (FAFSA) and the schools to which you apply.

- The FAFSA is the Federal Financial Aid form that allows qualified students access to many Federal Financial Aid programs. There is no charge to submit the FAFSA. Visit **<www.fafsa.ed.gov>**.

- The Expected Family Contribution (EFC) is the amount you and your family are expected to contribute to your education for one year. It is determined by the information you provide on your FAFSA. The EFC does NOT indicate how much financial aid you will receive from colleges. Colleges do not have to meet your financial need.

- Types of Federal Financial Aid include Stafford, PLUS and Perkins loans, Pell Grants, FSEOG, and Work-Study.

- A financial aid package that delivers at least 60% gift aid toward financial need is a good package.

- Even if you are not eligible for federal aid, you might be eligible for financial assistance from your state and/or from the college.

"To Do" List

- ❏ Start your scholarship search early

- ❏ File your FAFSA as soon after January 1st as possible

- ❏ Research educational loans and decide if they are right for you

- ❏ Save money for college

The Financial Aid Process

Financial Aid Forms

If you would like to be considered for financial aid, you need to know that **ALL** schools require the FAFSA form, and some of your schools may require the CSS/Financial Aid PROFILE application. Additionally, some colleges have their own forms. So you may have 3 different financial aid forms to complete!

Before reading more about financial aid forms, let us make two very important points:

1 **Know the Deadlines & Do NOT Miss Them**

All financial aid forms have deadlines. Be sure you ask your college Financial Aid Office what forms are required and when they are due. Each college has their own deadlines as to when financial aid forms must be submitted. If you fail to meet application deadlines you might be disqualified from aid for which you otherwise may have been eligible to receive. Though some financial aid is need-based, it is also "first come, first served." So, get your forms in as soon as possible!

2 **Parents & Students: File Your Taxes Early!**

You DO NOT need to file your taxes prior to submitting financial aid forms, so DO NOT miss a financial aid application deadline because your federal income tax forms have not been filed. Use estimated figures and return later to input accurate information. However, colleges may request to verify your financial information. To verify your financial status, a college will request to view student and parent income tax documents and W2's, so it is imperative that you and your parents file your taxes as early as possible (even if your parents are self-employed and usually file later). If a request for verification is made and your materials are not submitted, you will **NOT** receive a final financial aid package. So, file early!

The CSS/Financial Aid PROFILE® (CSS PROFILE)

What is the CSS Financial Aid PROFILE?

The CSS/Financial Aid PROFILE (we'll refer to it as PROFILE) is a financial aid application that many private colleges and universities require. You can find out if your schools require the PROFILE by visiting the College Board website at <**www.collegeboard.com**>. The PROFILE, a service of the College Board's financial aid division, is used to determine your eligibility for non-government financial aid, such as a college's own financial aid awards. The PROFILE collects detailed financial information and determines your financial need <u>differently</u> than the **Free Application for Federal Student Aid (FAFSA).** Unlike the FAFSA, the PROFILE takes into account whether or not your family owns a home. The FAFSA does not include your home when making the determination for financial aid. There is a charge for completing the PROFILE and you must register (through the College Board) before you can complete it. Register and complete the PROFILE online at <**www.collegeboard.com**>.

> **Financial Aid Forms**
> You may have to submit the PROFILE to <u>some</u> of your schools, but you have to submit the FAFSA to **ALL** of your schools.
>
> Hint

When to Submit Your PROFILE Application

If you wish to be considered for the best financial aid award possible, and your school requires the PROFILE, you should complete it as early as you can. Deadlines vary from school to school, so check with your colleges for their priority filing deadlines. You should submit your PROFILE to the College Board at least one week in advance of the school's earliest priority deadline. Complete the PROFILE early so you will be first in line when colleges award financial aid packages.

Does the CSS PROFILE Cost Money?

Yes, the PROFILE costs money and the fee usually increases each year. The current cost includes a non-refundable registration fee. You pay an additional fee for each school that requires your PROFILE. You may qualify for a fee waiver while completing your PROFILE online.

> **Register to complete the CSS PROFILE**
> **at**
> <**www.collegeboard.com**>
>
> Download a pre-application worksheet to assist you in completing the CSS PROFILE. DO NOT MAIL THE PRE-APPLICATION WORKSHEET – it is simply a guide to assist you in organizing your financial information before applying.

Free Application For Federal Student Aid (FAFSA)

The **Free Application for Federal Student Aid (FAFSA**) is the form the federal government uses to determine your eligibility for Federal Student Aid programs. As the name suggests**, there is no fee to complete or submit the FAFSA**. As you learned in the *Paying for College* section, types of Federal Aid programs include the Pell Grant, FSEOG, Work-Study and Stafford, Perkins, and PLUS loans. The form also collects financial information from you and your family. If you wish to be considered for Federal Financial Aid programs, you must submit the FAFSA each year you wish to attend college.

Once you have completed and submitted your FAFSA, you will receive a **Student Aid Report (SAR)**. The SAR indicates your Expected Family Contribution (EFC). The EFC is determined by a federal formula which is need based (based on student and parent income and assets). **Remember, the EFC is the amount of money the student and parents are expected to contribute to the cost of education for one year. The EFC does NOT indicate how much financial aid you will receive from a college.** In other words, you complete the FAFSA to determine how much you and your family can afford to pay and to qualify for Federal Financial Aid programs. As you learned earlier, colleges do NOT have to meet your financial need.

Where can you get a FAFSA?
- You can complete FAFSA on the Web at <**www.fafsa.ed.gov**> after January 1st.
- Paper versions of the FAFSA are available from your school counselor. Mail your FAFSA after January 1st.
- You can receive a copy of the FAFSA if you call 1-800-4-FED-AID.

> **Hint**
>
> **FREE** Application for Federal Student Aid
>
> If you are being asked to pay to complete or submit your FAFSA online, you are at the WRONG website. The FAFSA is free at:
>
> <**www.fafsa.ed.gov**>

When to submit your FAFSA
Do not wait until you are admitted to a college before you complete the FAFSA. As soon as possible after January 1st, complete and submit your FAFSA online at <**www.fafsa.ed.gov**>. The FAFSA is completed each year you plan to attend school. Renewals are submitted each year by online submission. In addition to financial and personal information, your FAFSA should include your college choices so the schools will receive your information directly from the federal processor. If you are applying to more schools than the spaces allotted on the paper form of the FAFSA, you can add more schools later (see p. 81). Remember, you must apply for financial aid each year you want to attend college.

Parent Information on the FAFSA

Students under 24 years of age are dependent on their parents by federal law even if they do not reside with their parents. If parents do not provide financial information on the FAFSA, a dependent student cannot be considered for aid. So, if you are under 24, single, not a parent who contributes more than 50% of the financial support of a child, not a veteran, and not an orphan or ward of the state, you must include parent information on your FAFSA. If you are a legally emancipated minor, some schools will allow a "dependency override" – meaning this requirement <u>may</u> be waived by the Financial Aid Administrator. However, this decision is completely at the discretion of the administrator. Call the school's Financial Aid Office if you have questions about your status.

Need Help Completing Your FAFSA?

College Goal Sunday is a free event that helps students and families complete the FAFSA! To check whether or not your state offers this event, visit <www.nasfaa.org> click on College Goal Sunday.

Completing the FAFSA

- **File as soon as possible after January 1st.** You do NOT need your completed tax forms to file - you may estimate using previous year's information. If you need financial aid to attend college, it is imperative to file as soon as possible to be considered for all Federal Financial Aid.

- **File online!** If you file the FAFSA on the Web, you will be weeks ahead of any paper submission. Your information will get to colleges much quicker, helping your chances of getting the best financial aid package possible. Assuming you are a dependent student, in order for you to file online, make changes or sign your online FAFSA, you <u>and</u> your parent need a **PIN**. You can request a PIN at <**www.pin.ed.gov**>. Keep your PIN in a secure place - you will need it to make changes and to renew your financial aid for subsequent years. **Note:** You will receive your PIN via email or through U.S. Postal mail as you request.

Hint

Signing Your FAFSA
Your FAFSA application will NOT be processed without signatures from both a parent <u>and</u> the student.

Paper version – Sign where indicated on last page.

FAFSA On the Web – You may print a signature page, sign and mail it to the address given **OR for faster results**, both student and a parent may sign electronically by registering for a PIN at <**www.pin.ed.gov**>.

- **Submit the FAFSA even if you do not think you will qualify for any Federal Financial Aid.** Sometimes being rejected for federal aid is necessary for receiving other financial aid, such as scholarships or grants.

- **Do not leave a field blank.** You can use a zero if the question does not apply to you.

- **Include yourself** in your parents' household size, even if you did not live with them the previous year (unless you are independent).

- **Sign** the application. If submitting online, sign the application by entering your PIN and parent PIN.

- **Keep a copy**. If you are filing the paper version, be sure to keep a copy for your records.

If you have questions, **The Federal Student Aid Information Center** is an excellent (and free) resource for assistance and information. For a quick response to your questions, you can speak with information specialists by calling toll-free 1-800-4-FED-AID (1-800-433-3243) or 319-337-5665 (not toll-free). TTY users may call 1-800-730-8913. If you are checking whether or not your FAFSA has been processed or requesting a copy of your SAR, you can access an automated response system at the same number.

Call the Center if you have questions about:
- How financial need is determined and aid is awarded
- Eligibility for federal student aid
- What schools participate in Federal Aid Programs
- Completing the electronic or paper version of the FAFSA
- How to get your PIN
- Making corrections or adding colleges to your SAR
- How your application information can be sent to a specific school

The Student Aid Report (SAR)

The submission of your FAFSA will generate your **Student Aid Report (SAR)**. The SAR is your official record that the federal processor received your FAFSA. You should receive a paper SAR within 4 to 6 weeks of submitting your paper FAFSA. If you filed your FAFSA on the Web, the process may take only 2 – 7 days! If you supply an email address, you will receive an email from the processor instructing you how to access your SAR online. When you receive your SAR, review it carefully! Review your Expected Family Contribution (EFC) and, if necessary, make any corrections.

Review your Student Aid Report (SAR) carefully. Check for accuracy on the following items:

- Student and parent Social Security Number
- Name, address and e-mail address
- Type of degree program
- Student income and parent income amounts
- The amounts on Worksheets A, B & C for both student and parent
- The number of students in college
- All of your schools are listed
- Housing plans (on or off campus)
- Were you selected for verification? If an asterisk is next to your EFC, you were selected for a process called verification. See explanation below. **

What if your SAR has been selected for verification? If there is an asterisk (*) after your EFC, it means your SAR has been selected for verification (one-third of all SARs are selected for verification). Your college(s) will review your SAR along with income tax documents to verify your financial status. If you are selected for verification, submit the information requested to the college's Financial Aid Office as soon as possible. **If you do not send the information requested, you will not receive a financial aid award from the school. This is why we recommend filing taxes early!

Call 1-800-433-3243 (800-4-FED-AID) if you do not receive your SAR in 4 to 6 weeks. You will be asked for your name, Social Security number and your date of birth.

Note your Data Release Number (DRN). Your DRN is the four-digit number located on the upper right corner of your SAR. You will need it to apply for aid to any school you did not originally list on your FAFSA.

Updating Your FAFSA Information

If you are completing the FAFSA on the Web, you may only make corrections to your information online. To update your information online, you will need your PIN and password.

Adding Colleges to the FAFSA

If you are applying to additional schools, you can add them to your FAFSA after submission and updates are made to your SAR. Once you receive your **processed** Student Aid Report (SAR) with all of the correct information (i.e. any updates to your financial information), you may update your list of schools by any of the following four methods:

1. **FAFSA on the Web**: Be sure to have your PIN and password. Go to the FAFSA website at <**www.fafsa.ed.gov**>. Click on "FAFSA Corrections" and replace the schools listed on your application with the schools you wish to add. (*Note: The original school codes on your SAR will be replaced by the new schools codes you add. The original schools will not receive your information if you make any subsequent changes to your application information*). Do not forget to **submit** the correction to your FAFSA information.

2. **Paper**: Replace the schools listed on your paper version of the SAR with the additional school code(s), and mail your SAR back to the U.S. Department of Education. (*Note: The original school codes on your SAR will be replaced by the new school codes you add. The original schools will not receive your information if you make any subsequent changes to your application information*). You will receive a copy of your updated SAR shortly and your SAR information will be sent electronically to the new school(s).

3. **Telephone:** You may call the Federal Student Aid Center at 1-800-433-3243 and request your SAR be sent to additional colleges by providing your Data Release Number (DRN). This number is located in the upper right corner of your SAR.

4. **Contact the Colleges:** Make your Social Security Number, name, and DRN available to schools so that they can obtain an electronic version of your Student Aid Report. The DRN is located in the upper right corner of your SAR.

The Financial Aid Process at a Glance

1

Register for your PIN at <www.pin.ed.gov>. A PIN is required to make corrections, submit your electronic "signature," etc.
Remember: *Completing FAFSA on the Web is easier and ensures quicker results!*

For dependent students, your parents also need to register for a PIN to sign the FAFSA on the Web. If you live with both parents, only one needs a PIN.

2

Gather all of your tax information and financial records. If you have not filed income tax returns yet, you can estimate.
Remember: *Even if you have not filed yet, estimate your information and make corrections later – after you file!*

3

To be sure you meet all deadlines, complete the FAFSA on the Web or the paper FAFSA as soon as possible after January 1st. Go to <www.fafsa.ed.gov> to apply.
Remember: *Federal aid is need-based, but it is also first come, first served!*

Do not forget to complete the CSS Financial Aid PROFILE, if your schools require it. Some of your colleges may have their own financial aid forms, too.

4

You will receive your Student Aid Report (SAR) as a result of your FAFSA submission. The SAR shows your Expected Family Contribution (EFC). If corrections are needed, make them and resubmit your SAR for reprocessing as soon as possible.**
Remember: *The EFC is the number used to determine your eligibility for federal Student Aid.*

** If your SAR shows you have been selected for verification, submit your completed tax information to your schools as soon as possible – include copies of the student and parent W2's and federal tax returns. If you do not send your financial information as requested, your file WILL NOT be processed and you will NOT receive an award from the school.

5

Once you have filed your taxes, update your Student Aid Report (SAR) by making corrections to the FAFSA on the Web or to your paper SAR.

Be sure all the schools to which you applied have your information.

6

Review your financial aid award letters and compare the amounts and types of aid from each school.

Summary

- Federal Financial Aid is first-come first served. Submit your FAFSA as soon after January 1st as possible!

- You must reapply for financial aid each year (after January 1st) prior to the academic year of enrollment.

- All schools participating in Federal Student Aid programs require the FAFSA. Some require the CSS Financial Aid PROFILE. You can find out if your schools require the PROFILE by visiting the College Board website at <**www.collegeboard.com**>.

- Check with your schools for deadlines and other financial aid forms or information that may be required.

- Do not wait until you have been accepted at a college to complete and submit your financial aid forms.

- **The FAFSA is processed faster if you complete it online.** The FAFSA will generate your Student Aid Report (SAR). The SAR will contain your Expected Family Contribution (EFC).

- The EFC is the amount of money student and parents are expected to contribute to the cost of education for one year. The EFC does NOT indicate how much financial aid you will receive from a college.

- Colleges do not have to meet your financial need.

"To Do" List

- ❏ File your taxes early, but complete the financial aid forms even if you have not completed your taxes – estimate and then update later.

- ❏ Complete your FAFSA as soon after January 1st as you can!

- ❏ Check your SAR for accuracy and update if necessary.

FAFSA FAQS

I started a FAFSA (Free Application for Federal Student Aid) application online, but cannot remember my password. How can I find it? If you forgot your password, you will need to complete another application. No one else has access to your password except for you. Your old application will be deleted 45 days after you started the application.

Can I save my FAFSA application on the Web? Yes! You can save your application online by selecting the save button at the bottom of the FAFSA page. The save button is listed on each page of the FAFSA online. Your initial application will be deleted 45 days after you saved the application.

What is the difference between the FAFSA and the Renewal FAFSA? Students attending school for the <u>first time</u> will complete the FAFSA. Once you have completed the FAFSA for the first time, you can complete the Renewal FAFSA to apply for financial aid for subsequent years. The Renewal FAFSA will save you time by using most of the answers you provided the previous year. Remember: You must apply for financial aid each year – complete the application each January.

I saved my FAFSA application on the Web several weeks ago. I tried to finish the application but, instead, receive a message stating that the application is not found. You can begin your FAFSA application on the Web and go back at a later time to finish. However, your application is only saved for 45 days. After that time, it is deleted.

How do I get a PIN to sign my FAFSA on the Web?
To apply for a PIN go to <**www.pin.ed.gov**> and select "Apply for a PIN." For dependent students, you and one of your parents will each need a PIN to sign the FAFSA on the Web. It takes only about 5 minutes to apply for a PIN. If you request that your FAFSA PIN be e-mailed to you, you will receive information to access your PIN via email within three days. If you want your PIN mailed via postal service, it will arrive in 7-10 business days.

Keep your FAFSA PIN! This is the same PIN you will use to make changes to your FAFSA application and to apply for financial aid each year when completing a Renewal FAFSA.

I forgot my FAFSA PIN. What do I do? You are given only one PIN. If you forget your PIN, do not complete another application to request a PIN. Visit the PIN request website at <**www.pin.ed.gov**> and request a **duplicate** PIN. If you apply for a FAFSA PIN after a PIN has already been issued to you, you will be told that you already have a PIN.

I have my FASFA PIN, but it will not allow me to sign using the PIN. I am sure I entered the correct PIN. What do I do? Go to the PIN website at <**www.pin.ed.gov**> and choose "Re-establish My PIN." Answer the questions and submit. After you re-establish your PIN, it should work. If not, you can contact Customer Service online or call The Federal Student Aid Information Center at 1-800-433-3243.

I completed a FAFSA application on the Web but used the wrong Social Security Number. How can I make this change? If you used the wrong Social Security number, you will need to submit another FAFSA application. Contact all the schools to which you applied and inform them which application has your correct Social Security number.

Whoops! I submitted two applications for the same filing year. What do I do? The first application that you submitted will be used. Your other application will be deleted.

How do schools receive my financial aid information?
Once your application has been processed, schools listed on your FAFSA will receive your information electronically, usually within 2 weeks.

On the FAFSA paper application, there is only room for me to list 4 schools. How can I add more schools to the application? There is room on the FAFSA for you to include four schools. If you are applying to more than four schools, you can add them to your FAFSA after submission and updates are made to your SAR (see p. 81).

I just made changes to a processed SAR and forgot to make a change. Can I make the correction now? You cannot make changes until your updated application has been processed and you have received your updated SAR. This should only take a few days.

I submitted a paper FAFSA application. Can I make changes to my SAR using the FASFA on the Web? You can make changes to your FAFSA application by using FAFSA Corrections on the Web even if you completed the paper version. You will need to have a FAFSA PIN in order to make changes online. You may request a FAFSA PIN at <**www.pin.ed.gov**>.

I submitted my FAFSA application over 2 weeks ago and still have not received my SAR. You can check the status of your application by choosing "Check Status of a Submitted FAFSA" at <**www.fafsa.ed.gov**>.

Can I sign my FAFSA on the Web using a PIN and have my parent sign on paper? You can sign electronically using your FAFSA PIN and print a signature page for your parent to mail, however, it will take longer to process your application using this method. Your application will be processed faster if your parent has a FAFSA PIN. To apply for your FASA PIN, visit **<www.pin.ed.gov>**.

How do I sign my Correction on the Web? Your FAFSA PIN acts as your signature to your online FAFSA application and you use your PIN to make changes to your processed application. If changes are made only to the student section, only the student needs to sign the form by entering a FAFSA PIN. If changes are made to the parent section, a parent signature is required. A parent can use his or her FAFSA PIN or print a signature page and mail it. Remember: Processing time is much faster if your parent has a PIN.

One of my parents already has a PIN. Can s/he use this to sign the FAFSA on the Web? If one of your parents has a PIN, s/he can use this PIN to sign the FAFSA, to sign the Renewal FAFSA, and/or make FAFSA Corrections electronically. Only one FAFSA PIN is given to each individual. You use this same PIN to complete future FAFSA applications.

What is a Data Release Number (DRN)? Your Data Release Number (DRN) is a four-digit number assigned to your application by the U.S. Department of Education. It is found in the upper right corner of the SAR. You will need your DRN if you want to add colleges to a processed FAFSA.

My family income from last year is much higher (or lower) than what we are currently earning. How do I add this information to my application? You must answer all questions on the FAFSA as of the date you are completing it. However, if you and your family have unusual or special circumstances that you believe are not shown on your FAFSA (such as unusually high medical bills or unemployment), visit or call the Financial Aid Office at the schools to which you are applying and explain. The Financial Aid Office at each school will determine whether the information you gave them will affect your aid award.

Making Your Decision

Acceptance to a College

You carefully selected your schools, made sure your application files were completed, submitted all of the necessary forms on time and then waited patiently for mail to arrive. And then the first letter arrives...

It is very exciting to receive a letter of acceptance! Yes, by all means, be very excited, but be sure to read the letter closely. Your letter of acceptance from a college will contain important information about decisions and deadlines. You may be asked to respond to many different questions from financial aid to student housing. If you have been accepted to multiple schools, make a note of the deadlines to respond. You can call the school and request an extension of the deadline if you need more time to make your decision. Discuss the letter with your parents and school counselor. If you have questions that were not answered in the initial letter of acceptance, contact the college and speak to an admissions representative.

If you are relying on financial aid to attend the college, **do not rush to make a commitment to attend the college before you review the college's financial aid award package**. When a school finally "shows you the money," you will know whether or not you will be able to afford the Cost of Attendance.

Wait Listed?

Some selective schools or programs receive more qualified applicants than can be admitted, so rather than being denied admission, applicants are placed on a wait list. Since wait lists tend to be large, the chances of a student being admitted from a wait list are usually small. If the acceptance letter states that you have been "wait listed" and you still want to attend the school, call and schedule an interview with an admissions representative. In some cases the school may move you from the wait list and you will be admitted. However, even if you are admitted, there may not be enough financial aid available to you.

If you have been placed on a wait list, consider attending another college (one where you have already been accepted and received a good financial aid package) so you can enroll for the fall semester with adequate financial aid.

The Financial Aid Award Letter

Typically, two to three weeks after you receive your acceptance letter (*assuming you have filed your FAFSA, and all other required financial aid forms*) you will receive a financial aid award letter from the school. Many of these letters are now accessible online. The award letter outlines the amount of financial aid the school is able to provide you for the upcoming year. If you are relying on financial aid to attend college, the aid award can determine whether or not you can afford the Cost of Attendance. There may be scholarships, grants, work-study and loans listed in the letter. Some of the aid may be renewable (meaning that you continue to receive the scholarship each year) and some may not – call and ask if you are not sure.

You must return your award notice to the school after indicating which types of financial aid you want. You may also have more forms to complete. Be sure you understand all terms of the letter so you can decide if you want to accept any, or all, of the financial aid offered. Here are the types of financial aid that might be available to you:

The following loans **MUST** be repaid
- Federal Stafford Loan-subsidized
- Federal Stafford Loan-unsubsidized
- Federal PLUS Loans – parent loan
- Federal Perkins Loans
- State, private, other loan programs

The following **DO NOT** have to be repaid
- Scholarships
- Federal Pell Grant
- FSEOG
- Institutional grants
- State-sponsored grants
- Work-Study or school employment

Sample Financial Aid Award Letter
Here is what you can expect to find on a typical financial aid award letter:

STATE UNIVERSITY
Financial Aid Office

Jane A. Student
27 Beverly Street
Portchester, ME 20000
Social Security Number: 123-01-0000

Dear Jane Student:

Congratulations on your acceptance to State University. We are pleased to offer you the following financial assistance to help meet your educational expenses for the upcoming academic year. This award is based on the information you provided on your financial aid forms and may be subject to verification and revision.

You may accept or decline any of the awards offered by indicating your response in the Accept/Decline column, signing and returning this letter.

Financial Aid Award

Type of Aid	Fall	Spring	Total	Accept/Decline
Federal Perkins Loan	$ 1000.00	$ 1000.00	$ 2000	A D
Federal Work-study	$ 750.00	$ 750.00	$ 1500	A D
Federal Subsidized Stafford Loan	$ 1313.00	$ 1312.00	$ 2625	A D
Federal Pell Grant	$ 2025.00	$ 2025.00	$ 4050	A D
Federal Supplemental Grant	$ 600.00	$ 600.00	$ 1200	A D
State Grant Program	$ 500.00	$ 500.00	$ 1000	A D
Totals	**$6188**	**$6187**	**$12375**	

Please sign this letter and return it to the Financial Aid Office by April 5th. If you are accepting the Stafford and Perkins Loans, you are required to read and sign Promissory Notes for each loan. You are also required to complete Entrance Counseling before loan funds are disbursed. Loan funds will not be disbursed without signed Promissory Notes or Entrance Counseling. You may complete the Promissory Notes and Entrance Counseling at our website <http://www.stateuniversity.edu/finaid/notes>.

_____   _____

Signature   Date

What You Should Know <u>Before</u> You
Accept and Return the Financial Aid Award Letter

Is the Award an Estimate or the Real Deal?

Some schools will send an estimated financial aid award based on your estimated financial information. If the word "estimate" is on your award letter, the final award may differ from the estimated award (it may go up or down). If you receive an estimated award, contact the school to find out more information about your final award. If you are selected for verification and you have NOT submitted your financial documents and other required information to the school(s), your award letter(s) are estimates, not the final package.

Be sure your school has your updated information.

Has your situation changed since you filed the FAFSA? Report any changes to the school. Outside scholarships, parental unemployment or illness, or a change in enrollment or family status could affect your award.

Note any deadlines – missing deadlines can be costly!

When choosing your school, you will need to inform the Financial Aid Office in writing of the award you plan to accept. If you do not respond by the date indicated, your financial aid award could be lost!

Common sense is good cents.

College costs money, but you do not want to start life after graduation with years of debt from large student loans. Be sure you consider your future career. How much money will you earn in your new profession? Are your job prospects good? Will you need a graduate or professional degree? The "value" of a college education after graduation sometimes depends on your major, so think carefully about loans. Is the value of the education at the college worth the Cost of Attendance and amount of loans you will have to pay back?

Select the college of your choice.

Once you know which college you will attend, it is good practice to let all of the other colleges where you applied know of your decision - this is important if you were accepted by several colleges. They can withdraw your application and open the slot to another prospective student without delaying the process for someone else.

When will you receive your financial aid? What can you use it for?
You will likely receive your financial aid money after the first month of school. If you start school in September, you may receive your money sometime in October. This is important to remember as you budget for school. You can use your financial aid money for most related educational expenses, including housing, food, transportation, supplies, personal expenses, books, and sometimes computers.

How will you receive your financial aid?
Your financial aid will be credited to your financial aid account at the school. Schools are required to disburse financial aid funds at least once per semester or trimester. If there is a surplus of money in the account after your bill is paid, the business office will reimburse you this amount, usually in the form of a check. With your permission, some schools will credit your bank account.

What about private scholarship money?
If you received a private scholarship (i.e. local, state, regional, national) the payment of this scholarship depends on how the group or organization wishes to pay you. Many scholarships are paid directly to the school and sometimes not until the second semester or trimester. The scholarship organization may require you to send a copy of your 2nd semester bill as well as a copy of your 1st semester grades. Additionally, many scholarships are payable for only one academic year versus those that are renewable each year. Renewable scholarships are payable over a period of time while others are awarded only once. For example, you may receive a $10,000 scholarship to be paid $2,500 over a four-year period as long as you are enrolled in school. Continue to apply for private scholarships throughout the time you are enrolled in school.

Remember that the amount of scholarships you receive from private sources may affect your financial aid award differently at each college. Some schools may lower the amount of self-help, and some may lower gift aid. Contact the institution to determine if and how your financial aid package will be affected by these scholarships.

Federal Loan Program Requirements
Unlike scholarships and grants, you must complete an application for each loan that you choose to accept. For Federal Perkins Loans, the college acts as the lender. For Federal Stafford Loans, you choose your own lender. Colleges will often give you a list of lenders from which to choose or you may choose your own.

All colleges and universities that receive Federal Financial Aid are required to provide students with **Entrance** and **Exit Counseling**.

Entrance Counseling is offered to first-time Federal student loan borrowers prior to the disbursement of the loan. Entrance counseling informs the student of the rights and responsibilities of the borrower (the student) including the conditions of the loan and the penalties of defaulting on the loan.

Exit Counseling is given to Federal student loan borrowers who are leaving school whether the student has graduated, is dropping out, or dropping below half-time enrollment status. Like entrance counseling, exit counseling also covers the rights and responsibilities of the borrower (the student) including the conditions of the loan and the penalties of defaulting on the loan.

INTERESTED IN FEDERAL STUDENT/PARENT LOANS?

The government pays the interest of Federal Perkins Loans and Federal Subsidized Stafford Loans as long as the student maintains at least a half-time enrollment status in college.

The government does **NOT** pay the interest on PLUS Loans or Federal Unsubsidized Stafford Loans. The interest of these loans is paid by the borrower and starts to accrue once the loan is disbursed.

A Loan Versus a Credit Card

You may be tempted to skip the loan paperwork and just use a credit card to pay for school – *not a wise decision*. You can pay off a student loan of $20,000 in 10 years with a maximum interest rate of 6.25% by paying $224 a month. Once the loan is paid in full, you will have paid $26,516 – and only $6,516 of that total is interest. To payoff a credit card debt of $20,000 in 10 years, with an annual percentage rate of 18%, you will have to make payments of $360 per month for a whopping total of $43,244 – and $23,244 of that total is interest!

Not Enough?

If you have read your award letter and discover that there is a large gap of unmet financial need between the Cost of Attendance and aid award you received, there may still be some options available to you to meet the cost.

1. Research more scholarship information at your high school. Sometimes scholarship money is still available. Talk to your school counselor.

Also, some places of employment offer scholarships to children of employees, so be sure to check out possible programs through your parents' employers.

2. Consult the school's Financial Aid Office for more information on the availability of payment plans.

3. If you are not certain that all of your circumstances were considered when the school made its decision, talk to the school's Financial Aid Office about your situation.

4. Check out other loan options that may be available to help you meet the cost of the school of your choice. However, be sure to consider the amount of debt you will be assuming when you graduate.

5. If your school is close enough, consider commuting from home rather than living on campus. This will save a great deal of money.

If the above options do not close the financial gap enough for you to afford to go to that college, choose another school! Since you have done your homework and applied to many schools, you will probably receive a better financial aid package from at least one of them, even if it is not your first choice. After all, the goal is to go to college, right?

College Cost Comparison Worksheet

Description	College/Univ	College/Univ	College/Univ	College/Univ
Tuition and Fees				
Room and Board	+			
Books and Supplies	+			
Personal/Other Expenses	+			
Transportation	+			
A **TOTAL COST OF ATTENDANCE**	=			
B (minus) **EXPECTED FAMILY CONTRIBUTION (EFC)**	_			
C *(equals)* **FINANCIAL NEED (A-B=C)**	=			
Grants and Scholarships				
Federal Pell Grant				
Federal SEOG	+			
College Scholarship & Grants	+			
Other:	+			
Other:	+			
D *(equals)* **TOTAL SCHOLARSHIPS/GRANTS**	=			
E **FEDERAL WORK-STUDY**				
Student Loans				
Federal Perkins Loan	+			
Federal Stafford Loan	+			
Other:	+			
F **TOTAL STUDENT LOANS**	=			
G **TOTAL FINANCIAL AID (D + E + F) OFFERED** *(Grants+ Work-Study+ Loans)*				
C **FINANCIAL NEED**				
G (minus) **TOTAL FINANCIAL AID OFFERED**	_			
H **UNMET NEED**	=			
TOTAL COST TO FAMILY **B + F + H** *(EFC + Loans + Unmet Need)*				

College Cost Comparison Worksheet

	Description		College/Univ	College/Univ	College/Univ	College/Univ
	Tuition and Fees					
	Room and Board	+				
	Books and Supplies	+				
	Personal/Other Expenses	+				
	Transportation	+				
A	TOTAL COST OF ATTENDANCE	=				
B	(minus) EXPECTED FAMILY CONTRIBUTION (EFC)	_				
C	(equals) FINANCIAL NEED (A-B=C)	=				
Grants and Scholarships						
	Federal Pell Grant					
	Federal SEOG	+				
	College Scholarship & Grants	+				
	Other:	+				
	Other:	+				
D	(equals) TOTAL SCHOLARSHIPS/GRANTS	=				
E	FEDERAL WORK-STUDY					
Student Loans						
	Federal Perkins Loan	+				
	Federal Stafford Loan	+				
	Other:	+				
F	TOTAL STUDENT LOANS	=				
G	TOTAL FINANCIAL AID (D + E + F) OFFERED (Grants+ Work-Study+ Loans)					
C	FINANCIAL NEED					
G	(minus) TOTAL FINANCIAL AID OFFERED	_				
H	UNMET NEED	=				
	TOTAL COST TO FAMILY B + F + H (EFC + Loans + Unmet Need)					

Summary

- Read your acceptance letter carefully and respond by the deadline, or ask for an extension to make your decision.

- If you are wait listed, and you still wish to attend the college in the fall, call and request an interview.

- If you need financial aid to attend college, do not make a commitment to attend the school before you receive a financial aid award letter.

- You will usually receive your financial aid award letter 2 to 3 weeks after your acceptance letter, assuming your financial aid documents were submitted by the deadline.

- Read your financial aid award letter carefully, accept or decline aid programs offered and respond by the deadline. If you miss the award deadline, your financial aid could be lost.

- If your award letter shows a large gap of unmet need, you may still have some options.

- Loans are serious financial obligations. Think carefully before considering loans.

- If you are not going to a college from which you have received the financial aid award letter, let the school know you will not be attending.

"To Do" List

❏ Carefully review all financial aid awards.

❏ Decide which college has given you the best aid award.

❏ Let the colleges know of your intention.

College Survival

College is Different

It is no secret that college is very different from the high school you attended. Requirements are more difficult, classes are often larger, professors are not as accessible as your teachers and the campus is bigger. The student body and student life are different, too. If you know what to expect, and what is expected, you can prepare yourself better for this exciting new experience. Most schools offer a freshman orientation to help prepare new students for the college experience. Be sure to attend the freshman orientation and ask questions.

More Students

You have to be a good student to be accepted to college, right? College classes are more challenging than high school classes and are organized differently. You may be in a class with over 400 other students! Not all classes are that large, but depending on where you go to school, you could be in a class with anywhere from 20 to 300 students – some students will be much older than you, some will have different beliefs, attitudes, majors, values, cultural backgrounds, etc.

Greater Expectations

Since college classes are usually larger and meet less frequently than your high school classes, you may not have as much contact with the instructor. Professors expect you to be independent and self-motivated. You will have fewer exams, papers and projects, but the material covered in class will be more challenging. You will be expected to attend all classes, understand and complete assignments on time and without reminders. Most college students keep a planner to record important test and assignment dates and to keep up with each class syllabus. College classes are more difficult, so managing your time well is very important - available time is not necessarily free time.

Get Help When You Need it

You will need to study more in college, so find a quiet space on campus, such as the library, and go often. If you are having difficulty in a class, do not wait until the last minute to get help. College professors do not stay on top of you like your high school teachers did. Your college success depends on your ability to remain motivated. In addition to teaching, professors have other responsibilities, so, unlike high school teachers, they may not be easily accessible after class. Most professors maintain office hours on campus. So, if you are having difficultly in a class, call or email your professor and make an appointment to meet. Do not wait until the day before a test or the end of the semester to get help!

More Opportunities

A college campus is like a small town and there are many things to do. Getting involved is key to survival at college. You can start by learning more about the campus community, organizations, and resources. Join a student group, like the outing club, play sports, or work on campus. Attend speaking and sporting events, programs and socials. Most colleges have study abroad programs that offer academic and cultural opportunities. Getting involved is a great way to meet new friends and explore new opportunities and experiences.

Beat Homesickness

Leaving your room, family and friends behind can be difficult. Stay in touch, but do not miss college activities to remain in contact with friends and family. You will feel more comfortable in your new environment by meeting new friends and becoming active in your new community. Do not visit home each weekend! The more involved you become on campus, the more comfortable you will become with your new life.

Do Not Get a Credit Card

It may be tempting when you receive all of those offers for pre-approved credit cards with 0% interest, but remember that credit cards are not free money – they are high interest loans! Many students do not understand how poorly managed credit card debt can impact their future. Our advice: Do not get a credit card.

Get Plenty of Sleep

It may sound like common sense, but it is important that you get enough sleep. Sleep is critical to maintaining good physical and mental health. The average college student needs 7-9 hours of sleep each night. Lack of sleep can negatively affect your memory, learning and reasoning abilities.

Eat Right

Forget home-cooked meals. College cafeterias offer all-you-can-eat greasy, fast foods. Limit these types of foods as they have little nutritional value. Make healthy choices such as the salad bar, sandwiches or foods that are freshly prepared, not fried. Have you heard of the "freshman 15?" Students on average gain approximately 15 pounds during the first year of college. Make smart choices and limit the amount of late night pizza deliveries. Limit your caffeinated beverages as well.

Get Active

Many schools charge students a fee to use the athletic workout facilities or gym. These fees are usually part of your Cost of Attendance (sometimes called a health fee or activity fee), so use the facilities! Being active makes you feel better, helps you manage anxiety and stress, improves your mood, helps you manage your weight, gives you a chance to socialize, helps you think better and gives you more energy.

Keep an Open Mind and Be Spontaneous

Explore other majors, careers and occupations, work in an area related to your interests, live on campus, volunteer your skills and time, or spend a semester studying abroad. Enough said!

College campuses have many resources for students

A college campus is like a small city and there will be many resources available to you right on campus. Though they may be called by different names at some colleges, here are a few on-campus resources students may find helpful:

- Bursar or Business Office
- Campus Security
- Campus Shuttle/transportation
- Career Center
- Center for Students with Disabilities
- Computer Labs
- Cooperative Education
- Counseling Center
- Dining Services
- Financial Aid Office
- Gay & Lesbian Student Organization
- Gymnasium or work-out facility
- Graduate Admissions Office
- Health Center
- International Student Organization
- Library
- Registrar
- Residential Life Office
- Student Activities Office
- Student Employment
- Student Center or Union
- Tutoring
- Women's Resource Center

What to Bring to College

Deciding what to bring to college can be a bit challenging. Remember you are going from your family's home to just one room that you will probably be sharing with another student. Here is a list of things that you may wish to bring along.

Personal Attributes
- ❑ Sense of adventure
- ❑ Sense of humor

Electronic Items
- ❑ Refrigerator
- ❑ Stereo (with headphones)
- ❑ Television & cable cord
- ❑ DVD Player
- ❑ MP3 player
- ❑ Telephone or cell phone
- ❑ Computer (if available)
- ❑ Alarm clock
- ❑ Desk lamp (not halogen)
- ❑ Power strip/surge protector
- ❑ Extension cord
- ❑ Fan
- ❑ _____
- ❑ _____

Laundry Items
- ❑ Laundry bag or basket
- ❑ Laundry soap
- ❑ Fabric softener
- ❑ Dryer sheets
- ❑ Laundry money
- ❑ Stain remover
- ❑ Bleach
- ❑ Sewing kit
- ❑ Iron and small ironing board

Bed & Bath Items
- ❑ Sheets, comforter & blanket
- ❑ Shower shoes (flip flops)
- ❑ Bath towels, soaps, robe
- ❑ Shower caddy (plastic tote for shower items)
- ❑ _____
- ❑ _____

Personal Items & Misc
- ❑ Clothes
- ❑ Backpack or book bag
- ❑ Address book & stationery
- ❑ Tape, scissors, pens/pencils
- ❑ Phone cards
- ❑ Organizer or planner
- ❑ First aid kit
- ❑ Tylenol or pain reliever
- ❑ Prescription medications
- ❑ Your insurance card and health Insurance information
- ❑ Flashlight
- ❑ Batteries
- ❑ Personal toiletries (toothpaste, toothbrush, deodorant, etc.)
- ❑ Hair dryer
- ❑ Sports equipment (football, soccer ball, basketball, hockey stick)
- ❑ Eating utensils (plastic)
- ❑ Cups and plates
- ❑ Can-opener
- ❑ Umbrella
- ❑ Message board for your door
- ❑ Anything to decorate your room
- ❑ Pictures of family and friends
- ❑ Throw rug
- ❑ Small trash can
- ❑ Paper towels
- ❑ Cleaning supplies
- ❑ _____
- ❑ _____

What you should leave home
- Pets
- Candles, incense, fireworks
- Expensive clothing & jewelry
- Air conditioner
- Prejudices

Glossary of College Terms

Articulation Agreement - An agreement between two schools that allows course credit to be accepted or transferred and be applied toward a degree or certificate.

Associate Degree - A two-year degree, like those conferred at community colleges or trade, technical or vocational institutes.

Bachelor Degree – An undergraduate degree that typically takes four years to complete for a full-time student.

Bursar or Business Office - This is where you go to pay your bill or ask questions about your bill.

COA or Cost of Attendance - The total cost of attending a college including tuition and fees, books and supplies, room and board, transportation and personal expenses.

College - A post-secondary institution that awards associate or bachelor degrees. Colleges can also be a division of a larger university, such as a college of liberal arts and sciences.

Commuter Student - A student who lives at home or off-campus and uses transportation to attend classes.

Core Requirement - A class that is required for a specific major or college.

EFC or Expected Family Contribution - The amount of money the student and family are expected to be able to contribute towards the cost of attending the college for one year.

Elective - An optional class that counts toward a degree, instead of one that is required.

Entrance Counseling - is offered to first-time Federal student loan borrowers prior to the disbursement of the loan. Entrance counseling informs the student of the rights and responsibilities of the borrower (the student) including the conditions of the loan and the penalties of defaulting on the loan.

Exit Counseling - is given to Federal student loan borrowers who are leaving school whether the student has graduated, is dropping out, or dropping below half-time enrollment status. Like entrance counseling, exit counseling also covers the rights and responsibilities of the borrower (the student) including the conditions of the loan and the penalties of defaulting on the loan.

FAFSA (Free Application for Federal Student Aid) - The federal government's required application for federal, state, and institutional financial aid.

Financial Aid - Federal, state, college, and private programs which help students pay for college costs. Financial aid can be in the form of grants and scholarships, loans, or work-study programs.

Financial Need - The amount of financial assistance a student needs in order to attend a school.

The formula for the financial need is:

Cost of Attendance
- <u>EFC (Expected Family Contribution)</u>
= Financial Need

Gap - The amount of unmet financial need in a financial aid package. The formula to determine a gap is outlined on page 59.

Gift Aid - Financial Aid sources such as grants, scholarships, work-study, that do not have to be repaid.

Grade Point Average (GPA) - A method used to evaluate the overall academic performance of students. A student's GPA is found by dividing the sum of grade points by the number of course work credits or hours. Grades are often measured on a four-point scale in which 4 = A, 3 = B, etc. These are called grade points. Total points are found by multiplying the number of hours for a course by the student's grade points.

Graduate Student - A student who has completed a bachelor degree and is working on an advanced degree such as a master or doctoral degree.

Greek Organizations - Social organizations (usually fraternity or sorority) named by Greek letters that students might join. These organizations often engage in social and charity events.

Liberal Arts - A school or course of study which focuses on developing students' general knowledge and reasoning ability instead of a specific career; the result is often considered to be a well-rounded, general education in the arts and sciences.

Master Degree - An advanced college degree earned after a bachelor degree, usually taking two years for a full-time student to complete.

Matriculate - To admit a student into a college degree program at a college or university.

Merit-Based Aid - Financial aid award based on a student's academic standing, extracurricular activities or other student characteristics that make the student an attractive applicant to the college or university.

Need-Based Aid - Financial aid award based on the income and assets of the student and parents.

Private Institution - An independent college or school that is not supported by state funds. Some independent colleges have a religious affiliation or are single sex schools.

Public Institution - A college or school supported by state funding.

RA (Resident Advisory) or CA (Community Advisor) - Student living in the residence halls to help answer questions for residents living on the floor.

RD (Resident Director) - A professional hired by the college or university who maintains the operation of the resident hall and supervises the RA/CA.

Registrars Office - The on-campus office that maintains your academic records including your transcript and class schedule.

Residence Hall (Dormitory) - A campus building where students live. Food service, social and educational activities are sometimes provided in residence halls.

SAR (Student Aid Report) - After completing your FAFSA form, you will receive your SAR. This lists your answers to the questions you provided on the FAFSA and gives your Expected Family Contribution (EFC).

Self-Help Aid - Financial aid such as loans (which must be repaid) and the amount that a family is expected to contribute.

Scholarship - Financial aid awarded for academic and other achievements or merit (music, athletics, etc). Scholarships do not have to be paid back.

Study Abroad - Educational programs where students go to school for some time in another country while making regular progress toward their diplomas or degrees.

Subsidized Stafford Loan – This is a Federal Student Aid loan program. Eligibility is determined by the FAFSA. The U.S. Department of Education pays the interest while the student is in school at least half-time. The amount of a subsidized loan cannot exceed the financial need.

Transcript - The official record of a student's educational progress; it may include listings of classes, grades, major area and degrees earned.

Undergraduate - Student working on a bachelor degree.

University - A large, post-secondary educational institution with a number of divisions, including graduate schools. Research is usually an important part of universities. Academic offerings are usually more comprehensive than at smaller colleges.

Unsubsidized Stafford Loan - This is a Federal Student Aid loan program. Eligibility is determined by the FAFSA. This program can fund students beyond the subsidized loan limit even if the student does not have demonstrated financial need. Interested begins to accrue upon loan disbursement.

Work-Study - A form of Federal Financial Aid where students earn money by working part-time at their college. Students apply for work-study by completing the FAFSA.

Notes

Notes

Notes

Notes

_____
_____
_____
_____
_____
_____
_____
_____
_____
_____
_____
_____
_____
_____
_____
_____
_____
_____
_____
_____
_____
_____
_____
_____
_____
_____
_____
_____
_____
_____

The Simple Guide to College Admission & Financial Aid

Notes

_____
_____
_____
_____
_____
_____
_____
_____
_____
_____
_____
_____
_____
_____
_____
_____
_____
_____
_____
_____
_____
_____
_____
_____
_____
_____